DATE DUE

HIGHSMITH #45231

In Memoriam

Virginia Shipman Bailey

1922-1990

This book is dedicated to the memory of my wife of nearly fifty years. She was a loving and faithful companion, the proud and caring mother of our three boys, and doting grandmother of our nine grandchildren and two great grandchildren whom she never had a chance to love, cuddle, and spoil.

Virginia was undoubtedly God's role model for a minister's wife. She not only loved and served her family, but she also loved and cared for the members of our congregation and the staff members with whom we served.

To me she was a loving wife, my best friend, wise advisor, devoted prayer warrior, tender critic, cheerleader, and helpful partner. She was certainly a living example of the woman described in Proverbs 31:28-31, "Her children rise up and call her blessed; her husband also, and he praises her; many women do noble things, but you surpass them all. Charm is deceptive and beauty is fleeting; but a woman who fears the Lord is to be praised. Give her the reward she has earned, and let her works bring her praise at the city gate." (NIV)

GOD'S PLANS
YOUR CHOICES

Autobiography of Elmer Bailey

God's Plans, Your Choices

Copyright © 2002. Elmer F. Bailey

Published by Elmer F. Bailey
            Memphis, TN

Cover design: Shédrianne L. Driver
Editor: Julia D. Flanagan
First printing, 2002

ISBN: 0-9702099-1-6
Subject Headings: BIOGRAPHY // AUTOBIOGRAPHY
Library of Congress Catalog Card Number: 2002101730

Printed in the United States Of America.

Unless otherwise indicated, Scripture quotations are from the King James Version (KJV)of the Bible. Other Scripture notations: The New International Version (NIV) © 1973 by International Bible Society, used by permission of Zondervan Publishing House.

CONTENTS

PROLOGUE

As you begin reading, listen to what God has to say about you.

My child...You may not know Me, but I know everything there is to know about you....(Psalm 139:1)

I know when you sit down and when you rise up...(Psalm 139:2)

I am familiar with all your ways...(Psalm 139:3)

Even the very hairs on your head are numbered...(Matthew 1:30-31)

For you were made in My image...(Genesis 1:27)

In Me you live and move and have your being...(Acts 17:28)

For you are My offspring...(Acts 17:28)

I knew you even before you were conceived...(Jeremiah 1:4-5)

I chose you when I planned creation...(Ephesians 1:11-12)

You were not a mistake, for all your days are written in My book ... (Psalm 139:15-16)

I determined the exact time of your birth and where you would live... (Acts 17:26)

You are fearfully and wonderfully made... (Psalm 139:14)

I knit you together in your mother's womb...(Psalm 139:13)

And brought you forth on the day you were born...(Psalm 71:6)

Used by Permission from Writer
Letter on File

FOREWORD

Dear Reader:

Elmer Bailey exhibited remarkable leadership skills through the years of his ministry as he endeavored with all his heart to help Southern Baptists build their congregations upon tried and true Sunday School principles.

Beyond that he has exhibited a servant heart towards the church and has been willing to make himself a servant of Christ in whatever aspect the church needed his skills, wisdom, resources, and time.

I have watched Elmer Bailey in times of difficulty and in times of prosperity. I have seen him go into a deep valley of sorrow as his precious wife went through a lingering illness and then on to Glory. Never did I see him waver in his faith or question the goodness of God.

This volume speaks of God's plan and our choices and how when we are given a choice to make, *Do we choose what we would want to do, or rather what God would have us do?* In each phase of his ministry, Elmer sought the Lord and strived to serve Him in whatever capacity he felt God's hand leading.

So many in our Bellevue congregation remember his leadership and dedication that helped Bellevue minister to people in the Memphis community through our Sunday School program. Particularly the young marrieds, college, career, and singles departments which were developed and administered through Elmer and Virginia's leadership over the years.

As you will learn, he has served as the associate of two presidents of the Southern Baptist Convention and was deeply loved by them both. Read on and be blessed by this man's life, as I have been.

Adrian Rogers
Pastor, Bellevue Baptist Church
Memphis, Tennessee

ACKNOWLEDGEMENTS

First of all I must thank Mrs. Ora Lee Love. When she read the first three chapters to help me with grammar and construction, she asked, "Elmer, what are you planning to do with this?" I told her I was writing it for my family. She replied, "You mean you don't plan to publish this?" She told me that would be a big mistake. "Your peers would thoroughly enjoy your story. Younger men and women in religious education work need to know the background of your life and history during your six decades of service." It was because of her encouragement that I ventured out into this uncharted territory.

Kevin Cochran coached me in the use of my computer. Many times I would have been lost without his brilliant mind and experience.

Dianne Mills, my secretary for twenty-one years at Bellevue was the one who bridged the gap between Kevin Cochran and my inadequacy with the computer. She knew how to interpret some of Kevin's help in plain English, and she spent hours repairing some of my errors. She has always made me look good! I see that to be the mark of a good secretary. I love her as a sister in Christ. She and her husband, Gordon, have carefully looked after me since my Virginia passed away in 1990.

Harold Souther, who led me to Christ in 1933, has supplied information about things, which had slipped my mind from our high school and Oklahoma Baptist University days.

Treva Belle Muggy helped me to remember the incidents, which led Harold and me to work in churches in South Central Oklahoma, during our last year at OBU. Neither Harold nor I could remember how it was we landed in Fox and Healdton, Oklahoma. At this time a young teenager, Treva Belle Muggy sang in my youth choir in Fox. Years later I located her in Broken Arrow, Oklahoma and she remembered much of the detail I needed.

Belton S. Wall Jr.'s book of the history of First Baptist Church, Downtown Jacksonville was invaluable to me as I reconstructed the Jacksonville years and the growth of the church.

I thank Jim Pirtle for allowing me to use excerpts from his document on some of the history of Bellevue Baptist Church. And I am so appreciative of my son Jim for his financial aid in publishing my book. Eloise Hatfield, who also served as my secretary at Bellevue, typed much of the manuscript, made corrections after my editing, and placed the text on computer disk.

Love Worth Finding Ministries handled the publishing of this volume, and I owe Bill Skelton and Cathy Allen a debt of gratitude for their expertise and competent counsel in getting this manuscript in its final form. I especially want to acknowledge the contributions of the marketing staff of LWF. Julia Flanagan, the editor, was courageously sensitive to each and every word of this book to ensure its grammar and content. God gave her spiritual insights, as well, which helped me redeem my book as a legacy to my family. Shea Driver, the graphic designer, met my every request with grace and smiles. She did a magnificent job of designing the cover and laying out the inside pages. Last but not least, Brandi Hayes was very helpful in coordinating the details for the printing of the book.

Dr. Adrian Rogers, my Pastor and dear friend wrote the Foreword of this book. He was most kind in his remarks about me. His words about the book are typical of his skill in the use of words.

PREFACE

Elmer Bailey is recognized as one of the most talented and effective church leaders in the Southern Baptist Convention.

Over the past half-century he has served in a wide range of ministry positions – religious educator, associate pastor, staff coordinator, church administrator, and musician. Elmer is a personable and caring individual and is abundantly qualified by education, experience, personality, and dedication to Jesus Christ.

In addition to being a distinguished graduate of Oklahoma Baptist University, he majored in religious education at Southwestern Baptist Seminary, Ft. Worth, Texas. Music captured his interest, and he has performed repeatedly as baritone soloist and music director.

His experiences on church staffs include tenures at First Baptist Church, Port Arthur, Texas; First Baptist Church, Jacksonville, Florida; Broadway Baptist Church, Knoxville, Tennessee; and Bellevue Baptist Church, Memphis, Tennessee, where he served twenty-two years with two Southern Baptist Convention presidents, Ramsey Pollard and Adrian Rogers. At Bellevue he built a dynamic Sunday School organization with weekly attendance up to 4,500.

During these years, Elmer also led countless conferences throughout the nation, including conferences at Ridgecrest and Glorieta Assemblies where he also served on the faculty.

Following his retirement, he formed Church Growth Basics, Inc., which has continued to help literally scores of churches focus on growth. He also answered a special call and served as staff coordinator at Germantown Baptist Church, Memphis, for several years.

Few if any, church staff persons have been more highly recognized among their peers than Elmer Bailey. He served as president of the Southwestern Baptist Religious Education Association, the Southern Baptist Religious Education Association, and president and metro board chairman of the

Metropolitan Religious Education Association. In 1988 he received the Distinguished Service Award for outstanding achievement from the SBREA.

Above all, Elmer Bailey is a deeply dedicated servant of Jesus Christ. Elmer's personal and spiritual attributes have made him a rare friend, father, husband, and Christian leader. He and his late wife, Virginia, were an outstanding team in every phase of their lives. A man of prayer and soul winning, his Christlikeness touches all who know him.

After more than forty years of association with Elmer Bailey as a colleague and personal friend, it was my privilege to recommend him as a recipient of Oklahoma Baptist University's Alumni Achievement Award, which he received in 1992. Here is a man abundantly representative of the historic Oklahoma Baptist University.

Sincerely,
Henry E. Love
Fellow Education Director
and Devoted Friend

A Word From The Author

I wrote my life story, not only for my family, but also to be a witness to others of the impact that choices can make in our lives, and to arouse a keen interest in others for the journey of finding and knowing God's plans. The plans are from God. The choices are ours. God's plans are perfect. The world's plans can be disastrous. And Satan's plans are condemning.

The first few chapters cover my infancy, early childhood, and pre-teen years. I had very limited knowledge of God or His plans, and even less understanding of the choices that would be mine and the ultimate results of my choices in later years.

God was planning my life long before I was aware. In fact, He had good and gracious plans for me, and not only for me, but also for all who claim Jesus as King of kings and Lord of lords.

As you read, you will discover a little boy who had a dreadful fear of death – to the point of obsession. And you will learn how he went from obsession to bitterness to anger to hatred and even resentment for those who were trying to help.

Blessings on you as you read. My prayer for you and myself is to "find God's plans" (Jeremiah 29:11-14) and "choose His plans" (Joshua 21:15).

Elmer F. Bailey
Winter, 2001

INTRODUCTION

MY PARENTS AND GRANDPARENTS

My dad, George W. Bailey, was born in Milan, Michigan, May 18, 1878 to the proud parents of Harmon and Emma Bailey. Harmon was the tallest officer on the police force of Detroit, at the time. In March 1901, he died of a heart attack at 47 years of age. I never got to know him since he died before I was born. My Grandmother Bailey then moved to the little village of Brighton, Michigan, where she lived for 26 years. I remember that she became quite feeble and my folks moved her to our home in Pontiac where she died in 1928.

My other grandparents died before I was born. All I know about them is that my mother's father, Bofinger, brought his family from Baden-Baden, Germany in the mid-1800s to a settlement in Canada, which they called Baden. It is just a few miles south of Kitchener, Ontario. The two grandparents are buried there. They had six children, two boys, and four girls. My mother, Carolina, was born in 1881. All of her sisters and brothers migrated to Detroit, Windsor, Ontario, and Port Huron, Michigan when they became young adults to look for work.

My mother Carolina found a job as a clerk at the S. S. Kresge Store in downtown Detroit. It was the first and only Kresge store, but later became a large national "five and ten" chain. She was a very young girl of approximately 18 and a long way from her homeland. This was her very first job.

One day a young electrician came to Kresge to fix an electrical problem. Mr. Kresge asked Carolina to show the young man to the electric control panel where the connections seemed to be shorting out. He fixed the problem, and then looked up at the girl who had helped him and introduced himself, "I am George Bailey. I graduated from Michigan State Normal and started to work today at Edison Power and Light Company. This is my first job." She replied, "Oh, we have something in common. I am Carolina Fredericka Bofinger. This is my first day here and my very first job."

There was more than just an electrical connection being made on this call! They began dating and before long she had him on the string. They were married on Christmas Eve, 1901.

Born to this union were three boys, Carroll in 1903, Donald in 1905, and surprise! – Elmer made his grand entry on December 24, 1916.

Soon after I was born, we moved from Lysander Street in Detroit to 28 Euclid Avenue in Pontiac, Michigan. Dad thought the growth of industry in the Pontiac and Oakland County areas would be a good place to start a business in electrical contracting. It proved to be a good thought.

I don't believe he realized how busy he was going to be with his "one man show." He was scouting for new business, studying blueprints of possible jobs, figuring all costs involved in building projects, and developing specifications and bids. Then came a bona fide contract, which usually led to negotiations. If he had just one job to do that would be a bundle of work, but jobs multiplied to the point that he had several jobs going at the same time. He had to have help, so he brought on an electrical engineer named Eric Gondas who could take most of the planning and preparation off his hands. With Mr. Gondas working in the office, Dad was able to be on the job sites.

Most of these jobs were schools, churches, industrial plants, and movie theaters. This required him to be away from home for days, and even months at a time. It seemed that I hardly ever saw my dad during these years. I knew he was working hard and making a good living for his family, but I missed him very much.

A BIG CHANGE IN OUR NATION

When the depression of 1929 struck with all its fury and frustrations, our family lost everything. The banks were closed and the future was dim. There was no cash available except what was in our pockets. Dad's business was at a standstill. People who owed him great sums of money couldn't pay. No money was available. Everyone was in the same fix. Some had fortitude to hang on and just exist, but many committed suicide, or went to pieces mentally and physically. It was a desperate time.

Then a miracle occurred. We were so fortunate. Mr. Gondas, who worked with my Dad, had saved enough money to start a business rebuilding and rewinding large electric motors used in power companies, water plants, and other types of industry. He was a genius at what had almost become a lost art. He hired my dad and trained him to do this tedious, but essential and much-needed service. You see, these motors couldn't be purchased and were not being manufactured. This business kept my dad and Mr. Gondas busy almost to the end of the depression. My Dad eventually retired from full-time work in 1939.

During the depression, all of us had to pitch in to make ends meet. Mother worked as a janitor in a church where she volunteered as a pianist. I helped her some and I also washed cars and hearses part-time at a funeral home to pay off a debt for my grandmother's funeral. I also sold *Colliers* and *American* magazines all over my neighborhood and at the Oakland Auto Plant. I would stand at the gate of the plant when the men were coming off the day shift and sell magazines. By the way, did you know that the Oakland automobile was the forerunner of the Pontiac? The Oakland plant became one of the many plants operated by Pontiac Motor Corporation.

Our Three Sons

God blessed Virginia and I with three sons: James Carroll, born in Port Arthur, Texas; Roger Bradley, born in Jacksonville, Florida; and Richard Ramsey, born in Knoxville, Tennessee. These fine young men brought joy and happiness to our hearts and to our home.

James Carroll

Our firstborn was James Carroll. As a child we called him Jimmy, and when he grew into adulthood, everyone called him Jim. He was a good baby but for one thing – he couldn't tell day from night because of his battle with colic for weeks and weeks. The doctor gave him medicine, but it didn't help. He finally wore it off, but it took a long time. We were so grateful to watch him grow and do all the fun things that babies do. Everybody loved Jimmy. The people in the church thought he was great, and of course, his mom and pop did too.

Jimmy was also outgoing. He smiled all the time and seemed to enjoy the attention people gave him. He loved to ride in the car. He didn't like staying home with a baby-sitter. At a very young age as he began to talk, he also began to sing. He could sing several hymns and children's songs. We were so proud.

I'll never forget when Jimmy was about four years old and he fell and hit his brow on the pointed edge of a table during Sunday School. The nursery workers found me and when I arrived, he was soaked in blood. We didn't have a first-aid room at that time, so we wrapped him up in towels and diapers and took him to the doctor. Jimmy kept calling out, "Just put a Band-Aid on it. Just put a Band-Aid on it." He didn't want a bandage around his head but a Band-Aid – he didn't get it. He got a bandage. It healed quickly and in a few days we were able to remove the bandage and there was no scar. I think he was a little frightened by the incident because he was hesitant to go back into the nursery room. I can understand, can't you?

One Christmas, we wanted to go to Virginia's home in Chattanooga. But first, we had to sing in a Christmas cantata. As soon as we finished about nine o'clock at night we left Port Arthur headed for Chattanooga. What an adventure! It wasn't long after that when we moved to Jacksonville. We moved in our little car and Jimmy rode in a basket in the back seat. What a sight! You can't do that today! The people in Jacksonville poured out the same kind of love to our little Jimmy and us. Everywhere we went, people loved him. He was such a personable little boy.

As Jimmy grew, he became interested in sports and played T-ball. In one of the games, he hit the ball and ran for first base. They got him out. The next time he came to bat he thought he had already been to first base, so he skipped it and went to second! Poor little fellow – he didn't understand. I also noticed when he was in the outfield that he would sit down and rest. If you want to have fun, go and watch the little guys play T-ball. Or better yet, volunteer as a coach! Those were happy times going to his games. It reminded me of the times I spent with my father.

Jimmy moved from being interested in baseball to basketball. As many times as I could, I attended his games. When he was in junior high school, he became interested less in basketball and played on the football team. He liked it and planned to play in high school, but unfortunately it was about that time we moved from Jacksonville to Knoxville. When he changed schools he didn't get registered in time to get into the football program. Jimmy was also active in all the youth activities of the church (as were the other boys when they came along).

After finishing high school Jimmy went to Oklahoma Baptist University just like his dad. He lived in a little home on Dr. James Ralph Scales' home property and took care of his horses (Dr. Scales was president of OBU at the time). This was his job to help with expenses for school. At the end of the third year, the OBU Board of Directors fired the President, Dr. Scales. When Dr. Scales was let go, Jimmy left at the same time. He was crushed because he was close to Dr. Scales. He became embittered toward the school and religious things. It took him a long time to get over that. He continued his education at University of Tennessee and received a degree in Business Administration.

After graduation, Jimmy took a job with Wallace Johnson in real estate development and other enterprises of the Johnson firm. He did well and after several years, Jimmy moved to Florida to work with an apartment development company. They had thousands of apartment complexes across the country. He carried many responsibilities and did a good job with each and every one. We were so proud of him.

At one point, the company bought a carpet mill and asked Jim to sell the inventory from the mill because they didn't intend to operate the carpet mill. They only wanted to sell the inventory, which amounted to about one million dollars. Jimmy didn't know anything about carpets, but he thought about the thousands of apartments they had all across the country where carpet had to be changed regularly. He suggested they sell the inventory to the apartment managers. And that is exactly what they did! It was only a short time until all the carpet was sold. It couldn't have been a sweeter deal for everyone and our Jimmy thought of it.

The company continued this with Jim in charge of supplying carpet for their units. Soon, the company expanded to other apartment developers and it became a big business. His hard work paid off and he was a great success in that business. Later, Jim moved to Denver, Colorado to start a new business

– "Community Interiors," which became a giant in the interiors industry. Jim is the President of this company. In his spare time, he takes care of his old dad's business affairs.

ROGER BRADLEY

Roger was our second baby boy and he was a fine baby. He wasn't quite as outgoing as Jimmy, but he was every bit as friendly and happy – he smiled a lot. We were so thankful he didn't have the colic like Jimmy! Roger was also interested in sports. After a few seasons, he graduated from T-ball to softball, and then he went on to play hardball.

I will never forget a trip Roger made with his mother while I was away in a conference. He was riding in the back seat and rolled down the window. Before Virginia knew what was happening, Roger threw out a pressure cooker Virginia had placed on the back seat. Of course, it was destroyed and I guess we all know that the rest of the trip was a little bumpy after that! He never tried a stunt like that again.

Roger went to grade school at Brownsville School in Knoxville. His favorite subject was Science. He decided to learn the Morse Code and make his own telegraph. He got a board and put the wire across it. It was a good idea until he plugged it in – it blew out all the lights in the school! In junior high school, Roger played trumpet in the band. That was his first experience with the trumpet and he did very well with it. At Central High School, he played first chair trumpet.

Roger's most exciting experience in high school was when he organized a rock and roll band. He had a lot of fun and the students loved it. However, the band didn't make the grade with the faculty or administration. After he graduated from high school, Roger went to Oklahoma Baptist University like his dad, and was there only a year and a half before he was drafted into the Army. Those were sad days for all of us because we knew that he would be headed for Vietnam.

He was sent to Fort Campbell for boot camp training, then on to Fort Louis in Seattle, Washington (this was a unit that trained the soldiers in helicopter radio and warfare). Time flew and he was shipped to Vietnam. When he returned, I asked about his first impression of Vietnam. He said the grass and the trees were so beautiful and green, but after they got to their area of combat, all they saw were muddy rice fields everywhere. He said it rained constantly. They had no buildings in which to sleep, so they had to find a dry spot along the edges of the rice fields. From there, they would fly in helicopters to wherever the enemy was located. This is where he first faced battle with 125 helicopter assaults.

Roger shared with me that he saw lots and lots of children, and they all seemed to be running loose without any adult supervision. At first they looked at the soldiers in amazement and fear, but Roger said they were kind to them and became friends with many of them. Even though they were in deep poverty, they were smart children. He enjoyed getting to know them. He joined the other soldiers and played with the children – even giving them gum and candy and toys. They also taught some of them to play ball.

Roger was the radio man in his unit and so wherever he went, he had his radio with him. He had opportunity to tune into some broadcasts from regular radio stations. One night in 1969, he was able to hear the story of Neil Armstrong stepping onto the moon. How thrilling this was for the men to hear! Some of the locals who were friendly to the soldiers were listening to the radio. An interpreter was also listening, but he couldn't understand what was going on. He tried to tell them, but they laughed. A man on the moon? Foolishness!

One day, a very dear friend of ours, Mae Powers, sent Roger a big box of Kool-Aid. They had no ice and couldn't really picture having Kool-Aid in warm water. They thought about putting it in their canteens, but they were advised not to put the Kool-Aid in there. They tried to figure out what to do, so they decided they would have some fun with it. They took all the Kool-Aid and put it in the water tower for the officers' showers. The officers never knew where that Kool-Aid came from. They tried to find out but never did.

Before the army sent Roger home, they flew him to Hawaii for some much-needed R & R. He was there 2 years before he was discharged and returned to Memphis. I will never forget the day he left to go to Vietnam and the day he came home. The day he left, we took him to the airport and watched him go through the terminal door to the plane waiting for him. As he walked down that sidewalk, his back was to us. As Virginia and I watched him go, we both had tears in our eyes. I didn't know until I interviewed him for this book that as he was walking down that sidewalk, he was crying out loud.

It was a different story when Roger came home. We were so happy and grateful to God for his safety, especially after all the danger he went through (he came home with no injuries). All he had were memories of the discomfort and fear of war. Now, we all know that our armed forces never really knew who the enemy was. Many of the Vietnamese were friendly to them and many were not. They had to find out the hard way. God prepared him and brought him home safely. How happy we were. What a celebration we had for him when he returned home!

Before I interviewed Roger for this book, he didn't want to talk about Vietnam. I was grateful that he seemed to really enjoy our talk and I believe he has been able to get rid of some of the bad memories from that time. He closed our interview with a story, which goes back to his youth, but it had an effect on him while in Vietnam. He said when he was in the Youth Choir at Bellevue, Dr. Tommy Lane introduced a song to the choir that caught Roger's attention and burned itself in his mind and heart. There was one line that he remembered clearly: "I know not where His island Palm fronds silhouetted in the air. I know I cannot live beyond His love and care." One day, after three nights of heavy combat, Roger was lying in the mud – cold, damp, and exhausted, yet praising the Lord and praying. He said he remembered looking out across the rice patty and seeing a tree line of Palm fronds against a fading sun. Shells and bombs were exploding in the background as the melody and words of that song again flooded his mind. I remembered a verse from Scripture, "Train up a child in the way he should go: and when he is old, he will not depart from it" (Proverbs 22:6).

When Roger got settled back into civilian life, he went to University of Memphis and studied radio production. After graduation, he went to work as a disc jockey for WHBQ-TV in Memphis. He worked there for about three years and met Betty Bartlett (she was a secretary for WHBQ). She was a lovely girl and he loved her very much. After dating for two years they decided to get married. God blessed their union with two children Brian and Shannon. Now, they have a granddaughter Parker, who is my great granddaughter!

God was working on Roger in those last few months at WHBQ. He felt God was calling him into the ministry. He surrendered to what God was asking him to do and was ordained by the Germantown Baptist Church. Later, he was called to pastor the First Baptist Church of Grand Junction, Tennessee. He had preached many times before for pastors who were temporarily out of the pulpit or for churches that did not have a pastor. Virginia and I were so pleased to see his potential. His first sermon was well organized and very good. We both felt our second-born was an outstanding, gifted preacher of the Word.

The Grand Junction church was known for not keeping its preachers very long (they changed about every two years). Roger decided he needed to leave and go to New Orleans Baptist Theological Seminary. We were so proud to see him graduate with honors. After graduation he came to the conclusion that God had not called him into the ministry after all. I don't know what led him to that point – whether he had mistaken God's leading or what. But, just as Virginia and I had done when he was born, we had to once again give him to the Lord. Roger made the choice and it was his to make. Since leaving the ministry, he has worked in the construction business and been quite successful.

RICHARD RAMSEY

Our third child, Richard Ramsey quickly became Ramsey to all of us (he was named after Dr. Ramsey Pollard and Dr. Pollard was emphatic about calling him Ramsey, so we followed his lead). Ramsey was a healthy baby – no colic once again! He kept his hours straight and didn't keep mom and pop up at night! Once in awhile he had a little tummy ache and cried a little, but very little.

Ramsey was a little shy and as a little baby, he was quite a Momma's boy. As he began to grow, he tried several sports like his brothers. He played T-ball, softball, baseball, and basketball. He never got into football any more than throwing it around in the back yard. He was an excellent golfer and could beat me any day of the week.

His next to last year in grade school, we moved from Knoxville to Memphis and he attended Maury for his last year of grade school. He turned out to be a whiz at spelling and he won the spelling bee championship for his first year at Maury. He qualified to go to the citywide spelling bee contest, but he failed to spell his first word in that contest. He was crushed. He had been working hard, but we tried to encourage him and told him how proud we were that he had won the school championship.

More exciting than the spelling bee was Ramsey's decision to make Jesus his Lord and Savior. When it came time to be baptized, he became a little frightened. He thought he might struggle in the water or get water in his eyes and hair. I told him not to be afraid, and took him on Saturday afternoon at 4 p.m. to practice. That seemed to give him a little more confidence. While we were practicing though, some people came in and saw us in the baptistery. They thought he was trying to swim in the baptistery and questioned us as to what we were doing. I tried to explain we were practicing and that he was to be baptized by Dr. Pollard on Sunday night. Maybe those people came the next night and learned I was telling the truth.

After his first year at Maury, Ramsey went to Bellevue Junior High. Ralph King was the principal of the school at that time. I asked Ramsey if he knew Mr. King very well and he said, "Too well!!" Seems he had more than a couple of visits to see Mr. King on the order of some of his teachers.

One of Ramsey's closest friends at the time was Bobby Mills. They did so many things together. One day, Bobby got into trouble at home and decided to run away. Without talking to his Mama and Daddy, Ramsey invited him to come and live at our house. They managed it so we never saw him. We saw some evidences that led us to believe something was going on but we couldn't put our finger on it!

One day I came home in the morning to get some papers I needed at the office. When I opened the kitchen door, I noticed the door to the closet off the kitchen closed when I came in. I went to the door and carefully opened it as I had no idea who was there. Behind some clothes in the closet was Bobby Mills. I asked what he was doing there. He said, "Sir, I don't think you know it, but I have been living here a week." Now, I understood why our grocery bill had mushroomed in a week. We also noticed the cokes were disappearing. Virginia was working at the hospital and I was working at the church, so neither of us was around during the day, and they managed to hide him at night.

I took Bobby by the shoulder and reminded him what a dangerous thing he had done and that he could put us into trouble if his parents thought we had kidnapped him. (Of course, they didn't do such a thing because they were dear friends of ours and they were embarrassed by what he had done.) I called Bobby's parents at once and they came to our house. They had no idea where Bobby was; they had been frantic about him. They were relieved by his return but they appeared angry at what he had done.

I don't know what took place at the Mills home, but I know what took place at the Bailey home. It was a wake-up call to Virginia and I that we needed to keep a closer watch on our children. From then on we arranged to be there when they came home from school. I grounded the boys for two weeks. They couldn't leave the house. God brought to my mind the Scripture "Spare the rod and spoil the child," so I applied the board of knowledge to the seat of learning for Ramsey, as well as Jim and Roger because they knew about it, but didn't tell anyone. It was years ago and now we joke about it.

Ramsey continued in sports at Bellevue and football became one of his favorite sports. He also played basketball and joined the golf team. In junior high, Ramsey didn't make very good grades except in Math. He really liked Math, and went on to take other math-related courses. After junior high, he followed in his brother's footsteps to Central High.

During high school, Ramsey began dating Julia Rowe. They dated for about five years, then decided to get married. They were a fine loving couple and God blessed that marriage with three children, two girls and a boy: Jill, Jodie, and Rick. They had a fourth child, Jonathan Paul, who was born premature and weighed about two pounds at birth. He only lived about a week. During that week we stayed close to the hospital and in the nursery where he was in an incubator and loved and nurtured him as much as we could. We had a brief, but real love affair with Jonathan Paul. We enjoyed the moments we had together for that week. Even though we were expecting it would come, we were all crushed when he died.

While Ramsey was in high school, he went to work for Kroger as a grocery sacker. Soon, he graduated to cashier, then they promoted him to the division accounting office. This was where his love of math came into importance. They liked him well and he worked there throughout his high school days. After high school, Ramsey went to the University of Memphis at night and worked at the Kroger accounting office during the day.

He then went to work for United Inns, which was an off-shoot of Holiday Inns as Data Processing Manager. His first assignment was to set up a computer system. He didn't have any experience in computers, so United Inns sent him to IBM school to learn how to set it up. He made good grades, then set up the system. They were happy with what he had done and kept him on for seven years. While he was in college he took several courses in business and computers, which helped him in the things God led him to do at his next job with a computer network business. He was in charge of training people to use the computers. He did such a fine job, that they established an arm of that business called the Bailey Training Group.

After two years with the training group, Ramsey went to work for Coca-Cola as Data Processing Manager in 1979. Soon, his job was changed from Data Processing Manager to Manager of Distribution and Logistics. It was during this time that Coca-Cola began taking over all of the bottling works that had been leased out to other companies. Ramsey had the job of bringing these stores under the umbrella of Coca Cola. He traveled all over the United States and to Austria. It was an interesting job to him, but he didn't like the travel, and he requested that the company let him settle down at home. They liked him so much that they agreed to his request and put him in charge of bottling works in the Memphis area. During the years he was with Coca Cola, in addition to traveling all over the country, he was located for some time in Atlanta and Jacksonville.

He retired from Coca-Cola after 23 years, then started a franchise business for Alpha Graphics in Spartanburg, South Carolina. Unfortunately, he went into that business at a time when Spartanburg was saturated with small print shops like Alpha Graphics. He closed the store and went to work for Commercial Computer Printing Network.

In many ways, the boys were the center of our lives. We all liked to travel and so we did a great deal. My work required me to travel a good bit, and the family went with me whenever they could. Virginia and I also participated in their school activities and were active in the Parent Teachers Association (PTA).

WE BECAME BALL FANS

When we moved to Knoxville, we became fans of the University of Tennessee Vols, especially football. We tried to go to every home game. Once in awhile we would take a trip to Alabama and Georgia to see them play. Of course, the Vols came through to beat Alabama and Georgia once in awhile. The boys would be decked out in orange and white and so was Granddaughter Leigh who was a Mississippi State fan (she would never cheer for the Vols when they were playing Mississippi State). She loved to travel with us.

FAMILY TRIPS TO GRAMPA BAILEY'S

Our family usually spent two weeks every summer at my dad's home in Hollywood, Florida. Over the years, all of the family would take vacations there except those working summer jobs. Dad had a beautiful cottage home and we would revel in the beauty of the poinsettias that surrounded the house from the ground to the roof line. It was a sight to behold. Dad also had several orange and grapefruit trees and we always cleaned out his fruit on our trips.

We had great fun. There were lots of stories told, pranks pulled, jokes by the dozen, and countless games of Monopoly. Often the boys would sleep on the beach. There was also great food! My dad had a friend named Claire, who was an excellent cook.

Every morning we headed about two blocks to the ocean where we would stay until about eleven o'clock. We would swim, snorkel, play beach ball and volleyball until it got too hot – then we headed to the house for lunch. On some days, those of us who liked to play golf would go to the golf course about seven o'clock in the morning. We would play until it just got too hot to play. When the boys were young, I could usually beat them, but it wasn't long before they were burying me in the sand!

A BRIEF TRIBUTE TO MY FATHER

Dad returned our summer visits by driving to wherever we were living at the time. He continued to drive until he was 90, and it scared us to death. He lived to be 97 and had never been a patient in a hospital until he contracted pneumonia just before he died.

Dad became a Christian listening on the radio to Billy Graham when he was around 86. I praise the Lord for that choice. He was so excited about it he called Virginia and me by phone to tell us how pleased he was for the witness we had given and apologized for being so abrupt and uninterested for so many years. We rejoiced with him and had prayer together. That was a happy time for me and for him also. He and his wife found a Methodist church in Hollywood and became very active there.

GRANDCHILDREN AND GREAT GRANDCHILDREN

I have nine grandchildren and two great grandchildren. Virginia and I were very, very proud of our children and grandchildren and now two great grand-children. Virginia went to be with the Lord before the great grandchildren came along. These children have been a tremendous blessing. What a great time we have when they all get together at family reunions. We had a reunion at Thanksgiving 2001. All of the children, grandchildren and great grandchil-dren were at the reunion except Roger. He had broken his leg the day before Thanksgiving and could not come.

Jim and Foy have three children: Leigh, Will, and Michael. The oldest grandchild Leigh Jones is the mother of my first great grandson named Colby who is about nine months old. Will is a student at the University of Colorado and an excellent trumpeter. Michael just graduated from high school and is going to New York Institute of Jazz. He is an excellent saxophone player.

Ramsey and Julia have four children: Rick is a graduate of University of Tennessee and works for Deere Landscaping in Nashville, Tennessee; Jodie is a hairdresser and a graduate of Plaza School of Cosmetology; Jill has a Masters from Sanford University and is an actuary with Blue Cross/Blue Shield of

Alabama; Stepdaughter Brandi is a university graduate (Brandi doesn't stay in touch unfortunately, so I don't know much else about her).

Roger and Betty have two children: Brian is a graduate of the University of Memphis and is a contractor in New Orleans, Louisiana; Stepdaughter, Shannon Shearon is a graduate of Sanford University and has a Masters from the University of Memphis. She is a ministry assistant at Germantown Baptist Church, and also the mother of my great granddaughter, Parker who is just over a year old.

They are all a dandy bunch of kids. I love them with all of my heart and am proud of every one of them. Their many accomplishments and mutual love and respect for one another have given me reason to be proud.

MY TWO NIECES

I have two nieces: Linda and Cheryl. Linda lives in Nome, Alaska. There are no roads to Nome, so there are only two ways to get there. You can either fly to Fairbanks or Anchorage, then take a helicopter. Or, you can dog sled. None of us were brave enough to do the latter, so we never had that experience. Linda is a nurse in a hospital in Nome and her specific duty is to fly with patients by helicopter to the Anchorage hospital for major surgery.

Cheryl lives in Albuquerque and every year the town hosts a huge hot air balloon festival. They have thousands of all colors and sizes. On one visit, I remember the balloons came down over her house and if you know anything about hot air balloons – they hissed. When they came over and began to hiss, her dog ran in the house and got under the bed. I still laugh when I remember that huge dog tucking its tail and running for cover.

Now, you have learned a little about my family. It's time to turn the page and begin reading: "God's Plans, Your Choices."

Chapter One

"Twas The Night Before Christmas"

On Christmas Eve 1916, my mother was up to her ears baking German Christmas cookies and a German Christmas cake called "Stollen". In the middle of the afternoon a crisis developed. Out went all the well-laid plans for Christmas – baking cookies and Stollen, exchanging gifts, decorating the tree, and more. Everything came to a complete halt. You see, my mother was pregnant with me and she went into labor about 3:30 p.m.

My older brother Carroll was commissioned to first call Dr. Simonton, then to call my Dad at work and tell him to get home! My brother Don was told to call Aunt Laura and ask if they (Carroll and Don) could come over to spend the night. What a Christmas Eve! All Carroll and Don could think about was *What's going to happen to Christmas?* Since they came along years before this Christmas Eve surprise, they were probably not too excited about what was taking the place of their Christmas!

I made my grand entry, just before Santa Claus, at 10:30 p.m. The next morning my aunts, cousins, and brothers gathered at our house for the traditional exchange of gifts. I took part in the party by crying, screaming, and doing whatever babies do to get attention. A few months after I was born, Dad got a job in Pontiac. This is where I lived until I went away to College in 1935.

A Trip I Should Not Remember

Much of what happened to me in my early years is a blur, but there is one thing I do remember. (My parents say I couldn't possibly remember, but the details are indelibly engraved in my memory.)

I was around two years old when my Grandmother Bailey's aunt died in Chicago. My parents decided we needed to go to the funeral, so Dad bought a new car for the trip. It was a 1917 Altar Touring Car with four doors and a canvas top. It had no heater or side windows and it was mid-winter. In place of side windows, isinglass (similar to plastic) curtains were fastened to the door frames.

All went well on the trip to Chicago thanks to my mother. Though the weather was chilly and there were few places to stop for food or gas, mother had brought quilts and blankets, and a basket filled with sandwiches, snacks, and two thermoses of coffee and milk.

This funeral was my first experience with death. I really couldn't under-stand it, and it was sure scary. My grandmother's aunt looked like she was asleep. It seemed like she could see and hear if she wanted to. I even thought I saw her move once. They told me that the next day they would bury the casket in the ground. You can't imagine what that did to me. It actually started an obsessive fear of death in my heart and mind, which obsessed me for the next fifteen years. I had bad dreams, hated songs about Heaven, and was afraid to go to sleep for fear that I would die before I awoke.

Now, the ride home was a far different experience. The weather had turned extremely cold. When we were just outside of Chicago, we drove into the face of a blizzard. We pressed on not knowing what to expect. And remember, there was no heater or defroster (this was before the day of these conveniences).

It got so cold that Dad pulled off the road and placed some of the blankets inside of the isinglass curtains. When he got back in the car, we were stuck in the ice and snow – helplessly stranded in the middle of nowhere. Fortunately, there were many others in the same condition and everyone was trying to help the other. After awhile the storm abated and some men helped Dad get the car going again.

Dad tried to cheer us up and said, "We will stop at the first tourist cabins we see, and we must get some gasoline soon." We drove for miles with no sight of tourist cabins, houses, towns, or filling stations. Before long, we began to worry that we would run out of gas in what seemed a wilderness. Well, finally it happened! The tank ran dry.

Dad became frustrated and mother tried to calm him down. She had us wrapped up in blankets and quilts, so we were fairly content. After a while a Michigan Highway patrolman came along with an emergency supply of gaso-line. He poured a five-gallon can of gasoline into our tank and told us we were only twenty-five miles to a town where we could find lodging, meals, and more gasoline. Dad tried to pay him for the gasoline, but he said, "This one is on the State." How grateful we were as we went merrily on our way. I don't remember anything else about the trip, but we arrived home without further difficulties.

EXCITING SUMMERS IN BRIGHTON, MICHIGAN

Summers during my pre-school days were spent with my grandmother in Brighton. It was always a fun time. She loved to tell funny stories about when she was a little girl. She also told me Bible stories about Daniel in the lion's den and Joshua and the walls of Jericho.

One of my favorite things to do was listen to records on her Victrola. This was a phonograph that you had to wind up by hand and it would run for several records. You could tell when it needed to be wound up again because the records would begin to run slower and slower until they finally stopped. She had lots of band music by Sousa. They were my favorites.

Grandma also had a stereopticon photograph viewer. This hand held device holds two identical pictures side by side. Looking at the pictures through the viewer gives the effect of a three-dimensional image. We spent many enjoyable hours looking at hundreds of pictures made for this viewer.

The biggest thing about Brighton in the 1920s was the Chautauqua shows. They came each summer with blaring bands, parades, clowns, balloons, crackerjacks, and animals. It was something like a circus. Grandma would take me to every performance down by the millpond.

I also remember watching the daily passenger train pass through town from Detroit going to Chicago. It was a long mid-morning train with passenger cars, dining car, lounge car, and mail car. The train was pulled by a big steam engine with bell ringing and whistle blowing at every intersection. There were two men in the cab of the engine – one was the engineer, who manned the controls, and the fireman who shoveled the coal on the fire under the boiler.

It was a daily ritual to walk two blocks to the station and watch the train pass by. Once in awhile it would stop to pick up passengers or let someone off. Otherwise it went through on the fly. Train time was a must for me every day.

TWO DIRTY TRICKS BECAUSE OF MY BIRTH DATE

The first "dirty trick" was my birth date! The worst time in the world for a birthday is December 24. No birthday parties, no cake, no birthday presents except those marked "Merry Christmas *and* Happy Birthday. This present is for both!" I never really had a birthday party or special birthday presents until I was married, but that's another story.

The second "dirty trick" was that I had to be six years old by the beginning of the fall term in order to enter first grade at Wisner Grammar School. This meant that I couldn't start school until I was almost seven years old! Most of my neighborhood friends were going ahead of me that September 1922. Thankfully, I wasn't alone to play with just the "little kids." Marvin Quick, Billy Hill, and a few others were in the same boat. But, I had one, important advantage. I was the oldest of them all, so I became the leader.

When it was time for me to start school in the fall of 1923, I had another problem. My mother wanted to take me to school, hold my hand, and hug and kiss me goodbye at the schoolhouse door. I know I should have been proud of this, but I thought it would be the most humiliating thing imaginable. I begged and begged her to let me go alone. I gave her several reasons why I should go alone, but she had been waiting several years to escort her baby boy to the schoolhouse. She wouldn't give up! Finally I told her, "If you won't let me go alone, I just won't go at all."

That did it! She started crying as if her heart was broken. (At the time I was too young to realize the strategy of the female of the species on little boys and on grown men.) I had to stop her crying. I said, "Aw, mom, please don't cry, I'll let you go with me, but please, please don't hold my hand, and if you must kiss and hug me, do it here at home before we go." So she kissed and hugged me and said, "Okay son, let's go"... and we did!

RINGING THE BELL AT WISNER GRAMMAR SCHOOL

I had no trouble adjusting to school. I thought I knew just as much as the "little kids" in my room. I was pretty little myself, but bigger than the others. My very best friend, Billy Hill, was a foot shorter than I was.

The big school bell that Mr. Kohen, the school janitor, rang every morning at 8:00 was of particular interest to me. Mrs. Kohen and my mother were very good friends and quilting buddies. One day when mom was going down to the Kohens, I asked her, "Mom, may I go to the Kohens with you? I'd like to talk to Mr. Kohen."

She let me come along, and suggested I might get a chance to play with their daughter Marvel. I didn't tell Mom about it, but that wasn't in my plans at all! I just wanted to talk to Mr. Kohen about the bell and my chances to come early one morning and watch him. In the back of my mind I was hoping that he might let me pull the rope. However I knew that this wasn't the time to think ahead.

We had the chance to talk and he told me that students were not allowed to enter the building until after the bell rang. "But," he said, "I will ask the principal." He did and the principal said okay, but with one word of caution: that I should not bring any other boys or girls with me. The Kohens lived about a half block from me and the school was across the street. Mr. Kohen said, "Elmer, you come to my house at 7:40 a.m. on the dot. Don't be late." I was so excited I was there ten minutes early! Now, I dreamed that one day he would let me help him ring that bell. To my surprise Mr. Kohen asked me that day if I would like to help him. I was overjoyed! There probably wasn't a kid in Wisner that didn't want to help ring that bell, and here I was a first grader about to have that opportunity.

Mr. Kohen showed me how to hold the rope, and just how far I must pull the rope before releasing and letting it go back to its original position. I noticed that if Mr. Kohen pulled the rope too much, the bell would go all the way over and ring three or four times. Mr. Kohen always kept his hands in control so this wouldn't happen.

After doing this for about a week Mr. Kohen said, "Well, Elmer would you like to ring the bell by yourself?" I said to him, "But what if I pull the rope too far?" He laughed and said, "I won't let that happen. You will do okay." What an encouragement, for I was afraid I might not do it right. Everything went well and I thought I was really somebody.

Mr. Kohen and I became good buddies. He liked to fish, so one Saturday he called and asked if I would like to go fishing with him. I told him I didn't know anything about fishing, and that I didn't have a pole or anything else I would need. He told me he had extra poles, and he would take care of everything else. Then he said, "You don't mind if I bring Marvel along with us, do you?" Well I wasn't ready for that. Marvel was a girl, and what if she showed me up? But Mr. Kohen had been so good to me I just couldn't say no. Well, we went to Silver Lake and the worst happened. Mr. Kohen didn't get a nibble, I didn't get a nibble, and Marvel caught three crappies! I never heard the last of that.

TRIBUTES TO SOME WISNER TEACHERS

I wish I could remember the names of all the wonderful, caring teachers and principals I had at Wisner. Many of them remembered my brother Don who preceded me at Wisner by eight years. I cannot begin to tell you what these people meant to me. They taught me so much more than just "readin', writin', and 'rithmatic". They taught me how to learn, how to live, and how to get along with others.

In 1927, my fifth grade teacher taught us how to make a crystal set radio. She told each of us to bring a Quaker Oats box to school the next day, along with a dollar bill or a dollar in change. She said she would furnish the rest. The next day she had plenty of copper wire, crystals, earphones, and other things we needed. We went home that afternoon with our own radio we had made with our own hands. They worked, too! WJR Detroit came in clear as a bell. One night I even picked up KRLD in Dallas and WGN in Chicago.

My sixth grade teacher arranged a field trip to Detroit. We attended a luncheon at the Book Cadillac Hotel and heard a lecture by the famed American author, Carl Sandburg. His lecture was way over our heads, but it was so exciting to meet an author of a book we were studying.

EARLY YEARS IN THE BOY SCOUTS

That same year, while I was in 6th grade I joined the Boy Scouts of America. What an impact this organization had on my life! I was a very shy person. Some even called me a sissy because I couldn't throw a ball correctly, and I wasn't that interested in athletics.

It was in the Scouts that I learned the basic tenets of morality, love and respect for my country, and the importance of the home. I also learned how to make fire with two sticks, cook a meal, play a bugle, and swim. I even learned how to catch and throw a ball correctly! What surprised my mother the most was that I learned how to make my bed and keep my cabin clean at summer camp. The Scoutmaster gave our cabin special awards if we passed cabin inspection. Each day we passed, a banner was placed on our cabin.

My grammar school years came to a close with two sad and extremely difficult events. Just before scout camp ended, my good friend Marvin Quick drowned in the lake where we all had so much fun. This rekindled my obsession about death. Marvin was a good swimmer, but he had gone a bit far from the rest of us. We never heard him cry out for help. He just silently went away. Needless to say, we were all crushed. The camp closed and we went home for Marvin's funeral.

Shortly after this happened, my Grandmother Bailey became very feeble and sick. Mom and Dad brought her to live with us. Soon it became evident that she was dying. I could hardly think about it. We were so close. I loved her very much. She was very good to me.

THE GREAT OBSESSION REAPPEARS

On my way home from school one day, I felt in my heart that my grandmother had died. Dad was waiting for me at the door and with tears in his eyes (I had never seen my dad cry before), he told me that grandmother had died. Then he hugged me and said, "We will never see her again."

My obsession about death began again. It was a dark time for me. This was the first time a relative very close to me had died. Mother tried to comfort me. For the very first time, she told me about Heaven and that my grandmother was already there because she loved Jesus.

Through the dark shadow of my fear of death, I could see little sunshine. And Dad's "We will never see her again" and Mom's "Grandmother is already in Heaven" seemed to be a paradox.

Grandmother was buried in Rural Hill Cemetery in Northville, Michigan where my Grandfather Bailey was buried. My mother and dad, as well as a brother of my dad (who died at age 7) were buried there. The cemetery is beautiful and very well maintained. Although it isn't a military cemetery, there are many Revolutionary and Civil War soldiers buried there. In fact, there is a plot next to the Bailey plot with several Civil War veterans. A large cannon of that era is the centerpiece for the plot.

Dad served in the Spanish American War, and served in Cuba and the Philippines. He was very active in veteran's affairs the rest of his life – visiting Spanish War veterans in the Veterans Hospital in Florida right up to a few days before his death. He was among the last four or five remaining Spanish American veterans when he died.

CHAPTER TWO

JUNIOR HIGH SCHOOL YEARS

For the most part of my last year at Wisner, my class wondered if we would go to Eastern Junior High, a school way across town, or to Lincoln Junior High, which was under construction in our neighborhood. Would Lincoln be finished in time? Well, labor strikes and bad weather made sure that we would make the long trek across town to Eastern. Being the only junior high school in Pontiac, Eastern was a large school. It was the old style building of large schools of that day. There were three floors, an auditorium, cafeteria, gym, and library that doubled as a study hall.

Of course, we were all disappointed, but I will never forget the first day at Eastern. The faculty had planned a big welcome for all of us and it was an exciting day. In grade school we stayed in the same room for all of our classes. Now that we were in junior high, we had homeroom and a different room for each of our classes.

A WRONG TURN ON THE WAY HOME FROM SCHOOL

At this time, Dad was working for Mr. Gondas – rewinding and rebuilding motors. Since his shop was downtown, Billy Hill, Marvel Kohen and I rode with him, then walked a mile and a half north to Eastern.

The school had two entrances and both looked identical. One day, I took the lead in heading home by going out the wrong exit. It all looked the same to the three of us, yet as we walked we saw fewer houses by the block. Finally Marvel said, "I believe we are going the wrong way." Billy and I stood our ground.

Soon, we came to a grammar school that we knew we didn't pass as we walked to school each morning. A lady was out in front and we asked the way to downtown Pontiac. She pointed in the opposite direction. We turned on our heels and bashfully headed in the right direction. Billy and I had to admit we were wrong. I heard Marvel laughing to herself and saying "Told ya." We knew that everyone in our neighborhood would know the story before bedtime.

MY INTRODUCTION TO MUSIC

There were two things that I liked about Eastern Junior High: English and Band. First, Mrs. Gondas was my English teacher (the wife of the man with whom Dad worked). The first day of class, she recognized me and said some nice things about me to the class and how much she liked my folks. She made English so exciting. I had never made good grades in English, but now I did in her class. Some teachers just know how to teach!

The other thing I liked about Eastern was Band. Dale Harris, the band director at Pontiac Central High School, was initiating a program to make band an academic subject in both junior and senior high. He came out and helped us get started and enlisted an assistant to teach band at Eastern. He announced that the School Board was giving him another assistant to teach Band at Lincoln Junior High when it opened next year.

This is where I really got my start in music. I learned more about music during my years in junior high and high school band, than I learned in college. We were all on equal footing in the band, for we were all beginners. Some of us moved up into leading positions. Before the year ended I had moved to first chair trumpet.

DEATH BRINGS DEEP DESPAIR

The most disturbing thing that happened that year was the rather sudden death of my mother. She became very ill the day before Christmas. The doctor thought she had indigestion, but the medicine he had given wasn't working. Dad and I went through the motions of exchanging gifts while we nursed her. By the afternoon, the doctor said we needed to get her to the hospital. He called an ambulance, and Dad rode with her. I rode in the car with my brother Don and his wife. We stayed at the hospital most of the night while the doctor called in specialists who did all kinds of tests.

The next morning, my mother was in critical condition. The doctors said her heart was nearly twice the normal size. They said her indigestion was common and that they would do all they could for her. The medicine she took seemed to relieve the pain and she slept most of the night. In the morning there was a marked change. She was alert, and even smiled and apologized for spoiling Christmas for us. The next day, however, she started downhill and she died on New Year's Eve. It was a very hard experience for me.

I was a "Mama's boy," and I couldn't see life without her. Dad was so busy that I hardly had any time with him. And church wasn't a help either. For as long as I can remember I went to church every Sunday morning and sat on a pew by the piano. Mother brought me when I was a baby in a basket crib, and that was my Sunday morning place for the next thirteen years. To be honest, I went to church only to be with my mom.

I don't recall anything that the preacher, Dr. Creswell, had to say. I presumed he preached the Gospel, but I never saw that it applied to me. As a little child I busied myself with coloring books and toys, and as I grew older, I tried to listen but was bored. I hated the music for so much of it was about dying, or about Heaven. That old obsession about death and dying was still there, as well as the bad dreams. In many ways, I was a miserable kid and the death of my mom only made things worse.

Dr. Creswell conducted mom's funeral. His text was from Mark 14:8: "She hath done what she could." His message was more of a eulogy than a sermon. He talked about what a good woman she was (and she was a good woman). He talked about her faithfulness as the volunteer pianist for the church (and she was faithful). On many occasions, she made sacrifices to be present for services or rehearsals. Dr. Creswell said, "If anyone could get to Heaven by doing the right thing, Carolina Bailey was that person. I know she's there in that place that Jesus has gone to prepare. She is with Jesus and her loved ones who have preceded her in death."

Now the question began running through my mind: *How good do I have to be to get to heaven?* I knew that I wasn't good like my mother!" Did Mr. Creswell tell the truth? No one could be honest and preach a sermon for my funeral like he did for my mother.

From that point on, I resolved to never go back to that church. I was bitter and hurt. I was perplexed and mad at God. Why would God take my mother away from me? If He knew anything, surely He knew I needed my mother.

PROBLEMS IN SCHOOL

My personality began to change, I started skipping school, and my grades dropped. The only subject in which I excelled was Band because I had it the first period. After that class, I would sometimes just go home. Every now and then I would get on the trolley and go to Detroit, either to see my brother Carroll or to see one of my aunts. In order to get by with this I had to lie, and one lie led to another. This wasn't anything like the kind of boy I was before my mother died.

Mrs. Gondas was the first to take notice about what was going on in my life. She knew far more about me than I could imagine. She talked straight and firm to me, but at the same time, kind and gentle. I thanked her and told her I knew she was right. I promised to do better.

About the same time the principal asked to see me. He showed me grade sheets and notes I had forged with my dad's writing. He asked me who signed them and I remembered my promise to Mrs. Gondas. With guilt and remorse, I said, "I did, Sir." He responded, "With your low attendance records, poor grades, and these fraudulent notes, I have no choice but to turn you over to the Juvenile Court." Though it may not appear this way, Mrs. Gondas had nothing to do with the principal's action. My talking with her was just a fortunate coincidence.

The next day the notice came from Juvenile Court, a copy to me, my dad, and my brother Don. (Don and his family moved in with us after mom died.) I was really up a tree. I didn't know whether to run away or what. How could I face my dad with these things? I expected him to blow his top, though he had never disciplined me before; Mother was always the one.

Well, Dad wasn't the first to see the notice. Don was the first to come home from work and read his letter. He ranted and raved at me, swearing and calling me stupid. He warned me that Dad would rip me apart when he came home. He frightened me, but I knew his temper was more related to his alcohol problem, than me.

When Dad finally came home, he took the letter and sat down to eat his supper. I noticed he didn't eat much supper. He said, "I'm going to my room to rest awhile. I've had a hard day. Elmer, you come to my room and wake me in a half-hour. We need to talk." That was the longest half-hour ever! I knocked on his door right on the minute. He said, "Come in and sit down. I need to freshen up a bit and I'll be back in just a few minutes." I didn't know if he was trying to prepare me or prepare himself for the inevitable.

A Bonding With My Dad

Finally he came back. He quietly told me that he was disappointed in me and reminded me the charges were serious. He then said something that not only startled me, but also gave me a fresh understanding of my dad. He said, "Elmer, I feel that I am as much to blame for this as you. I have woefully neglected you for years, and especially in these days since your mother died. Please forgive me, and let's give it a new start. I'll arrange my schedule at work so that I can be home an hour earlier. At the same time, as much as possible, I will not work on Saturday or Sunday so we can spend some time together. I want you to know that I am proud of you and love you very much. I want to be best friends with you." We hugged and cried, and agreed that this was a good experience. I promised that I wouldn't skip school any more and I wouldn't write any more notes on his behalf.

A Significant Day In Juvenile Court

The next step was our appointment with Juvenile Judge Camille Kelley. She went over the serious charges and wanted to know what I felt. My dad interrupted and told her what he had told me and the promises we had made to each other. The Judge was pleased and said she wished more of her cases were so easily settled. "However," she said, "because of the seriousness of the charges, I will require you both to return to my court every sixty days to report progress on the promises you made to each other. You will make arrangements with my court clerk for the court appearances."

After the second visit she dismissed the case and thanked us for the progress we had made. No one was happier with the whole thing than my dad and me! It worked out very well. Our new relationship was exciting for both of us. Dad discovered if he left the office an hour early, and stayed away on Saturdays and Sundays, that he could get more done than on his former routine. We started doing many things together.

FIRST DAYS AT LINCOLN JUNIOR HIGH

At the beginning of my last year in junior high, our class was able to finally move into Lincoln Junior High. We were so excited! (When Lincoln was opened, it proved to be one of the largest junior high schools in the state.) I studied hard and got my grades back to an even better average than before my difficulties. I also was able to maintain my first chair trumpet position in band.

And speaking of band, with the good training we had received at Eastern, we already sounded much like the Pontiac High School Band. Dale Harris, whom I mentioned earlier, directed our first concert at Lincoln. For those of us completing our junior high work, it was our last concert at Lincoln.

Graduation from Lincoln was a big event. In spite of the difficult days early on at Eastern, I graduated with honors. It was exciting to think we were headed to high school.

THE EXCITING SUMMER OF 1931 WITH DAD

Two events occurred the summer of 1931, which were highlights of my life. First, my bonding with my dad. We enjoyed several new experiences. He was on a bowling team and asked me to join. We bowled every Thursday night and Dad took me with him on other nights, as well as Saturday afternoons to give me pointers on the game.

We also took a road trip. Dad was National Commander of the United Spanish War Veterans and that summer they were to have their National Convention in New Orleans. He invited me along as his unofficial aide. He thought I could still wear my Scout uniform, but I had outgrown it. We both felt it wouldn't be right anyway since I was no longer a Scout. The next day Dad took me downtown and bought me a navy blue sport jacket, two pairs of gray slacks, two white shirts, a tie, and a pair of black shoes. This would do for my "uniform," as well as dress-up clothes for several years. We drove to New Orleans from Pontiac in a 1930 Model A Ford Coupe. And here's the best part of the trip – Dad taught me to drive!

ANNUAL HIGH SCHOOL BAND CAMP

The other exciting event of the summer was the annual band camp at Walled Lake State Park. We had lots of fun swimming and boating, but we gave most of our time to Dale Harris. The moment we arrived, he stated his clear expectations of us. He explained that it wasn't only an honor to be a member, but also it was an academic subject which required home work in music theory, personal practice, five one-hour sessions for rehearsal, and teaching of music fundamentals.

Mr. Harris told me that he wanted me to try out for first chair trumpet when I returned to school because his #1 trumpet player graduated. This was a big challenge since Pontiac Central High Band had been recognized for several years as the leading high school band in the state. All of the incoming freshmen, including myself, wanted to do our best so we could be #1 again.

CHAPTER THREE

BEAUTIFUL CAMPUS BECOMES CONCRETE JUNGLE

One of the most scenic spots in Pontiac, Michigan, was the campus of Pontiac Central High. I don't know why it needed the "Central" in its name, since it was the only high school in Pontiac at that time. The classically designed three-story buildings were the centerpieces of a beautifully designed campus. A lovely park filled with pathways, trees, and flowers reached toward the skyline of the city. I have never seen a college or university campus to compare with it.

How sad that those graceful buildings, flowers and trees are gone now. The rolling hills have been leveled and the school replaced with one-story buildings. Much of the parkland is now paved with concrete to provide parking for the hundreds of cars driven by students, faculty, administrators, and visitors. In 1931, few faculty and administrators drove cars to school – most came by city bus or streetcar. Not more than a dozen students had cars. Quite a change, wouldn't you say?

This overwhelming place was the center of my life for the next four years. Those were good times. Mr. John Thors, Jr. was principal at Lincoln and became principal of Pontiac Central in 1931, which was my first year there.

SENIOR HIGH SCHOOL DAZE

I will forever remember the teachers who made a dramatic impact on my life and a fellow student who led me to Christ. That decision made the most remarkable and wonderful change in my life.

The first days of school were a nightmare, trying to find the way from building to building, and room to room was quite confusing. But first, we had registration, which was in the auditorium. We filled in paper work and selected the possible course of study, which for me was College Preparatory. We then received what seemed to be tons of instructions regarding lockers, activity tickets, cafeteria coupons, things we should not do, and things we must do, etc.

AN INFLUENTIAL ADVISOR AND FRIEND

My faculty advisor, Maynard Dudley, assisted me in selecting specific classes in my schedule. He was an older teacher who had a good sense of humor and a genuine concern for students. He treated all of us as if we were his children. He also was my math teacher and pulled my feet from the fire by giving me personal help.

Mr. Dudley graduated from the University of Michigan. He was a teacher, high school principal, and school superintendent in several cities. He came to Pontiac High as principal and served for eleven years. Mr. Dudley was also very interested in music. When he first arrived in Pontiac, he was disturbed that the city didn't have a high school band. So, he organized the first Pontiac Senior High School Band in 1911 and served as band director and principal for several years. Around 1920, Mr. Dudley decided to go back to the classroom and teach math. I am grateful to have had this wise, loving, and grand gentleman as my advisor, math teacher, and friend.

TRIBUTE TO MY HIGH SCHOOL BAND DIRECTOR

The #1 class on my schedule was Band. What a privilege to learn and play under Dale Harris' direction. He was a superb musician, talented director, strict disciplinarian, and teacher unequaled. I practically worshiped the man. He was building a band, but more importantly, he was working toward developing character and a commitment to responsibility.

The entire band shared my devotion to Dale Harris. Everyone respected him, but not all loved him. Most of us couldn't understand all that he was trying to do for us. Some resented his rigid discipline, not recognizing that he was trying to teach us good character traits. At the time of this writing, Mr. Harris is retired and living in California. He attended many band homecomings over the years. You should have heard the many tributes of those who were influenced by this man!

Well, I followed Mr. Harris' suggestion and tried out for first chair trumpet. I thought there was no way that I, as a freshman, could win that position over upper-class pupils. Of the four who tried out for first chair trumpet I was the only freshman. When Mr. Harris gave the results, I couldn't believe my ears. I was first chair! As soon as I could, I phoned Dad at work and gave him the good news. He was so proud. He said, "Let's celebrate tonight. How about a bowling session?" I was on cloud nine. I guess the adrenaline was flowing when we got to the bowling alley because I beat him one out of three games. I had beaten him before, but very few times.

The next day, Mr. Harris explained to the first chair winners, that we didn't own that position permanently. Every week the person in second position could challenge the one in first position. One week from that date we would have a play-off, and the better of the two would assume first chair.

THE BEGINNING OF A NEW ERA

I held the first chair trumpet position for my whole freshman year and into my sophomore year. Then, competition arrived. Just after school started in the fall, a young fellow arrived in Pontiac from Nebraska. He was a trumpet player. As the custom was, Mr. Harris placed him in the last chair of the third trumpet section. This new student then had the privilege all of us had of challenging the person above him in his section. I noticed him working his way up and it wasn't long until he was sitting next to me in second chair of first section. Now, before I tell you what happened next, let me tell you about this young man named Harold Souther.

Harold was a dedicated Christian and member of the First Baptist Church of Pontiac. From the moment Harold came to sit next to me in band, not a day went by that he didn't talk to me about his church. He invited me to some of the activities. He even told me his church had a little orchestra that could use me. He tried to witness to me and I gave him the cold shoulder. I rudely told him to leave me alone – I wasn't going to his church or to any church.

At the time I was playing with a little jazz group in beer joints and small bars on the weekends. I usually didn't get home from these "gigs" until the wee hours of the morning. Dad tried to get me to stop, but I felt I needed the money (it was very little). At least, it gave me a little spending money so I didn't have to keep asking Dad. To be honest, I hated the job and didn't like the people I was associating with – it was the pits. I wasn't making very good decisions at that time.

Thankfully, Harold didn't give up on me! He became less aggressive in his approach, but he didn't give up. Every once in awhile he told me he was praying for me. No one had told me that before. Why would he want to pray for me? He didn't know what was going on in my life. I guess I was still bitter in my heart toward God, the church, and religion.

AN INVITATION THAT CHANGED MY LIFE

One day Harold came to me with an urgent appeal to help his orchestra at church. They were planning to do a number for church, but they only had two trumpets, and desperately needed three. Harold said, "I know that you have told me to leave you alone and I have tried to respect that. But if you will come and help us this one time I will never ask you again." I thought, *Maybe this is a chance to get him off my case.* I told Harold, "Okay, I'll help you this one time, but you be sure and keep your word about leaving me alone." He told me his folks would pick me up at 9:00 a.m. on Sunday. This would give us time to go over the music, and practice with the group.

I started to back down because nine o'clock was very early for me on Sunday morning. He pleaded some more and told me that his mother wanted me to have dinner with them after church. He had already told me at another time about his mother's home cooking. It sure had been a long time since I had a home-cooked dinner. He had me where he wanted me!

Sunday came and they picked me up. The music was simple and I didn't need much time to learn it. The other trumpet player arrived and we went over the music with him. In ten minutes we were ready. I asked Harold, "Now, when do we play?" He answered, "eleven o'clock." It was 9:30. I said, "What do we do for an hour and a half?" "We go to Sunday School," he replied. I had never been to Sunday School!

A New Era Arrives

I didn't really want to go to Sunday School, but I wanted to be polite. After all, I was his guest. He took me to a room full of teens – many I knew from school. Among them was Marvel Kohen. I hadn't noticed before, but the "ugly duckling" I knew from grammar school had become a beautiful girl. She seemed to be very glad to see me and welcomed me to her church. Then, she introduced me to her boyfriend.

There also were several band members in the Sunday School class. Each told me they were happy that I could help them out on this Easter Sunday. I then met the teacher Ralph Pardee. Harold told me that Mr. Pardee had been very helpful to him. He had given Harold many opportunities to use his trumpet in "Christian service." I really didn't know what "Christian service" meant, but I was soon to find out.

Mr. Pardee taught a lesson on the Resurrection of Christ. I guess I believed in the Resurrection, however, I didn't see how it applied to me at first. As he talked, he began to change my outlook on life, and in particular, the Christian life. I began to see the reality of Christ's promise of eternal life to those who would trust in Him.

My Salvation Experience At Seventeen

After Sunday School we went into the church service. We played the hymn "Christ the Lord Is Risen Today" arranged for trumpet trio. God was using Mr. Pardee, Harold Souther, and the pastor, Dr. Savage, to simply but clearly explain how a person could be saved.

Dr. Savage began right where I was – in my sinful state. He read Romans 3:23: "All have sinned and come short of the glory of God," and with great emphasis he continued, "But the GIFT of God is eternal life through Jesus

Christ the Lord." Then, he asked us to silently place our own names in place of the "all" in the verse. He demonstrated this by reading the verse with his own name. "Now," he said, "we will all say it together and you put your name in place of the 'all.' " Next, he read John 3:16 and did the same thing – asked us to substitute our names for "the world" and "whosoever." He took one more step. He read Romans 10:13 and asked us to substitute our own name for "everyone who."

After explaining what Jesus has done for us – not because of anything we could do, or pay, or be – he went on to explain that Christ died to save us from our sin, arose from the dead to give us victory over death, and simply "by His grace" if we received Him, He would save us! In closing Dr. Savage asked everyone to bow their heads, close their eyes, and answer the question, "If you died today would you know you would go to Heaven, with your sins forgiven?" He said, "If your answer is 'no' I wish you would raise your hand and by doing that you are saying 'I don't know where I would go or be if I died tonight. Dr. Savage, pray for me.' "

He kept pleading, I wanted to raise my hand but I guess it was pride somehow keeping me from doing it. I felt a hand on my shoulder and my friend Harold Souther at my side saying, "Elmer, you are struggling. I can tell by the tears in your eyes and the way you are gripping the pew. Raise your hand and let Dr. Savage pray for you." I did what Harold asked me to do! Then, Dr. Savage prayed for several of us to make the decision to let Jesus come into our hearts. He also prayed that God would give us assurance about our salvation.

The blessed moment finally came when he extended the invitation for us to come and receive Jesus. He said, "If you are not ready to make that decision and you need more help, come and someone will help you. If you want to trust in Jesus, this is the time. Come now, as we sing." Harold whispered, "I'll go with you if you wish." I whispered back, "I know I want to do something about this, but it's all so new." Harold said, "I know it's new, but it's something you need to settle now." I didn't need any more time, I was ready. Down to the front I marched with Harold by my side.

Dr. Savage spoke words of encouragement to all who came forward, then he said, "After the closing prayer, those who came forward will go to a quiet place where someone will help you to make any decision you need to make." Harold was right by my side when we walked to what they called the "inquiry room." Harold sat across from me and using his Bible, he led me to a point of decision. After reading scriptures and praying, Harold asked me, "Elmer, would you like to pray and ask Jesus to come into your heart and save you? If so, I'll help you." He led me in the sinner's prayer. After I prayed, he asked, "Elmer, what has happened to you?" I replied, "I guess I'm saved!" Harold said, "There's no need to guess about it." He gave me scriptures on assurance and we got up from our knees. I knew I was saved – born again! Remember the old obsession that had plagued me for years? Well, it was immediately gone. And, it has never returned.

MY BURDEN FOR MY DAD

Now, my burden was for my dad. I began praying for him to have the close relationship with God that I had found. He wasn't receptive. It seemed he had mellowed some, but the Masonic Lodge was still his crutch. He seemed satisfied that in their rituals he could find peace and security. Many of my friends at the church were praying for him. Even, the Highway Heralds at school were praying for him. Dr. Savage and his wife were praying for him. God gave me the assurance that one day my dad would be saved. Dr. Savage made it clear that I must not give up on my dad – just as Harold didn't give up on me.

A NEW RELATIONSHIP WITH GOD

Praise the Lord! This was the beginning of a new life for me. I had so much to learn. I will forever be grateful for Harold Souther. He never gave up on me! Our friendship blossomed into a life-long relationship. I lived at his home much of the time. His mother and father became my extended family. His brother Billy had graduated from Oklahoma Baptist University and was at Southwestern Baptist Theological Seminary. In time to come, Billy became my hero and mentor in preparation for my career. Of course, this was all in the future and you will read more of Billy Souther in future chapters.

I know this experience of finding Christ has taken a great deal of space in this chapter, but it deserves it. This was the greatest time of my life! I know that I am not all God wants me to be, but I am a long way past where I was before that epochal Easter Sunday of 1933.

CHAPTER FOUR

FINDING OUT ABOUT CHRISTIAN SERVICE

Do you remember a man by the name of Ralph Pardee, who I mentioned in chapter three? My friend Harold said Mr. Pardee encouraged him to use his trumpet in Christian service. I didn't know what that meant, but I soon found out!

Mr. Pardee had a heart for God and a love for youth. He stayed on the alert for people like me who needed to get to work for the Lord. Over the years hundreds of young people were enlisted in various projects. Some are now missionaries, preachers, and musicians. Others are using their talents for God in secular professions. Praise God for Ralph Pardee, a humble man of God who was fully dedicated to his calling to recruit and train young men and women, then put them to work for the Lord.

It was the summer after I trusted Christ and Mr. Pardee was calling for volunteers to preach and conduct Vacation Bible Schools for a week in August in northern Michigan. Harold urged me to sign up, but I told him I didn't know anything about Vacation Bible School, and I surely knew nothing about preaching! He told me we would be trained to do Vacation Bible School at First Baptist the next week, and when it came time to preach, then we would give our Christian testimony. Harold and I made up a team – he would give his testimony Monday, Wednesday, and Thursday nights. He asked me to give my testimony on Tuesday night. On Friday night we would have a Gospel concert.

I had not yet told my dad about being saved and now I felt I should before going out on this trip. Now, Dad didn't go to church. He didn't say anything about me attending First Baptist with my friend, nor did he encourage me. In fact, when I told him I was saved, he expressed his bitterness about church and told me I would be better off not getting so involved.

I was deeply hurt. I couldn't understand why he would say such a thing. I related this to Harold, and he reminded me of my own rebellion towards church in the days before I was saved. He said, "Your dad is probably not saved, and he doesn't understand what has happened to you." He prayed for my dad, and then asked me, "Have you witnessed to him?" I told him I hadn't and was afraid. He replied, "Elmer, you must," and he gave me several Scriptures about witnessing for Christ. I told Harold I would try. Harold said, "Don't be afraid, God will help you."

The first chance I had to be alone with Dad, I asked him if he was a Christian. He quickly answered, "The Masonic Lodge is my religion and that's enough for me. I don't want to talk to you about religion." I said, "I respect what you say, but Dad, I'm going to pray that you'll make Christ your Lord and Savior and that you will discover the peace and joy I've found in Him." He answered not a word. I remembered Harold's words, "He just doesn't understand." I continued praying for him and occasionally speaking to him about the Lord, but there was never any progress.

After our VBS training, Harold and I joined Mr. Pardee and two other young people and headed for Elm Grove, Michigan (don't look for it on a map). It was a small rural community on the Au Sable River made up of a few small farms, a schoolhouse, post office, and a general store. There were no churches and no paved roads.

We pulled up in front of the schoolhouse, which was a one-room building with a path leading to the outhouse. The school was our home and meeting place for the week. We unloaded our gear and Mr. Pardee took Harold and I to the house where we would have breakfast every morning. He introduced us to our hosts and took us back to the schoolhouse. Then, he took the other team to a similar community about twenty miles from us.

Harold had been to Elm Grove on a previous year, so he knew a few of the people. He also knew what we had to do, and so I looked to him as my leader. When we arrived, it was late on Monday afternoon and we had to prepare for the service that night. We also needed to plan for VBS the next morning. Harold picked out some songs we could sing from a song sheet – for the most part they were choruses and songs we could sing with trumpet accompaniment. We had no idea who would show or how many. Mr. Pardee had contacted some people before we arrived, and they were responsible for getting the word around the community.

The first night, we thought no one was going to show as it was beginning to get dark. But, people began to arrive and we had about fifteen people the first night. We had no electricity, but they were so eager to hear us and grateful we had come that they brought lanterns. Some drove to the meeting in cars, and a few came by horse and wagon.

The order of service for Monday night was as follows:

- Harold and I opened the service with a duet.
- I led in prayer, then taught the group two songs: "Every Day With Jesus" and "I Have The Joy, Joy, Joy, Joy Down In My Heart."
- I sang "No One Ever Cared For Me Like Jesus."
- Harold gave his testimony.
- Harold played a trumpet solo: "How Great Thou Art."
- We gave an invitation.

We told them about VBS and tried to figure how many we could expect. The family with the horse and wagon had several children. Another family said their children would come. We asked the ladies if they would bring some cookies and cold drinks. Two said they would bring cookies, but as for something cold to drink, they said they would bring paper cups and we could pump water from the well.

Before Harold and I retired to bed, our hosts told us that breakfast would be at 6:00 a.m. (not early for Harold, but quite early for me). We had to walk to the farmhouse about a mile to eat breakfast, and then walk back to the schoolhouse to get ready for VBS. Now, let me remind you that it was August, and although we were in northern Michigan, it was hot. The farmhouse had no screens and the windows were open wide – flies were ready to eat before we were! The food looked delicious and smelled even better, but we could hardly eat for the flies. How were we going to do this every morning? Well, somehow we managed. By the time we were back to the schoolhouse, our tongues were hanging out and we couldn't wait to prime the pump for water.

For Vacation Bible School, we had twenty-three children aged five to thirteen. We opened each session with:

- "The Star Spangled Banner"
- Salute to the American flag
- Pledge of Allegiance to America
- "Holy Bible Book Divine"

- Pledge of Allegiance to the Bible
- Prayer
- Bible Story
- Play time and Bible drills to learn books of the Bible
- Memory drill to learn a verse a day
- Fun games, such as musical chairs

After VBS that first morning our host came by in a 1929 Ford Model T pick-up truck to take us to lunch. On the way, he hinted that we might enjoy helping him load hay in his barn after lunch. Now Harold's folks had a big vegetable garden, and he was accustomed to hard work like tilling the soil and chopping the weeds. But, I was a city boy and had no such experience. I believe that was one of the hardest afternoon's work I can remember. My hands were covered in blisters when we finished. But, no time to whine because we had to wash up and be at another place at 6:00 p.m. for supper.

Our host gave us some towels, and pointed to a river, the Au Sable, which flowed nearby the schoolhouse. Harold had some soap, so we took a nice bath and were ready when the lady came to pick us up for supper. Now, this was a nice clean home with screens on the windows. And the hostess had prepared finger-licking fried chicken with all the fixings.

We were more prepared on Tuesday night for they had told us the day before that the night service would be at "dark thirty," which meant thirty minutes after dark. This was Harold's night to lead the music and my night to give my personal testimony which I had never done publicly before. I was scared to death, but the Lord was with me and gave me just the words I needed. I prayed someone would be blessed. When I gave the invitation, a farmer came to be saved. He was an older man and after the service he told me that he had been running from the Lord for years. I know he was blessed, but what a blessing his decision was to us!

The rest of the week was much the same through Friday night. Mr. Pardee came about 11:00 p.m. to take us home for the weekend. Then, we returned the next week for another round of Vacation Bible School and revival services. We had similar experiences and blessings on all the mission trips.

The next summer, Mr. Pardee found a place for the Gospel Heralds Quartet to serve as leaders for Vacation Bible School and nightly Bible study sessions in two small churches near Bay City, Michigan. We had a wonderful two weeks playing our instruments and singing. Jim Savage brought maturity to the group, as he led the Bible Study sessions each night. How we praised God for the opportunity to train and be a blessing at the same time! We didn't know it, but God was preparing us for a lifetime of blessings in His service.

Time began running out on my high school days. I was now in my senior year and my thoughts rushed ahead to prepare for the next four years. Harold and I had already made up our minds we were going to follow in his brother Billy's footsteps to Oklahoma Baptist University.

TWO THINGS I TAUGHT HAROLD

I learned a lot of important things from Harold, but I want you to know that I taught him a thing or two, as well. Soon after we became close friends I taught him to drive my dad's 1930 Ford Coupe. I remember the fun we had on our double dates in that car. Because Harold didn't know how to drive, I had to drive and he got to sit in the rumble seat with his girlfriend Mary Louise Stout. I had to teach him to drive so that Virginia Stapleton and I could enjoy the rumble seat together once in awhile.

I thought I was really in love with Virginia. She was pretty, happy, and fun to be around. I just knew she was the one for me – we even went steady for more than a year. When I went away to college, though, my good friend Jim Savage stole my gal. How brokenhearted I was! I thought that I'd never find another like her. I didn't know it then, but God had something better for me down the road. I even had to go through another heartache before I discovered the jewel of jewels who blessed my life and my ministry all of her days.

Another thing I taught Harold was how to eat in a restaurant. That may sound silly, but let me remind you that we were living in the depression and eating out was rare. Harold's papa was an employee in the automobile industry and during the depression those plants were closed for long periods of time. Harold's family had only one source of income for years. They had a large vegetable garden, and when those vegetables ripened, they sold them at the farmer's market in Pontiac.

Though times were hard for my family, as well, I had an allowance for school lunches and spending money. Sometimes I would go downtown to eat lunch at the Woolworth Five and Dime. They served a good hot lunch for only seventy-five cents. My favorite was the hot beef sandwich with mashed potatoes and gravy. One day I had a little extra money, so I invited Harold to be my guest. He said, "I don't have any money." I replied, "You are my guest." Believe it or not, Harold had never been to a restaurant; I had to help him order. He said, "Just order the same for me," and so we enjoyed our hot beef sandwiches. We had to run back to the school to keep from being late.

MY SENIOR YEAR IN BAND

Mr. Harris asked me to switch from trumpet to baritone during the last year of band because I was the only baritone in the band; I had no competition. I had grown a little tired of playing second chair to Harold in the trumpet section, so it was quite easy to make the transition. I also liked the counter melodies, which the baritone part carried.

At the end of every year the band gave a concert. My dad had never attended any of these concerts until my junior year. It pleased me that he now took a great interest in the band. He even went to all the ball games when we marched and played. Though this made me happy, I was never able to get him to go to church with me. On many occasions, I tried to talk with him about his relationship with God, but each time I got the same answer, "The Masonic Lodge is my religion."

Graduation Day in June 1935 was an exciting day for Harold and me. Pontiac Central had been good for both of us.

HELPFUL HIGH SCHOOL TEACHERS

Mr. Harris, my band director and Mr. Dudley, my math teacher were the most significant teachers during my high school years. Also, I must give honorable mention to one of my English teachers, Mrs. Rubert. She had the unique ability to make those dusty old books come alive. When I was failing her course because of my slow reading, she helped me after school. She was a sweet and caring lady. I am ashamed that I joined my peers in calling her "Peg-Leg Rubert." Years before she had lost one of her legs and she wore a prosthesis. She limped slightly, but believe me, she didn't limp when it came to teaching.

THE PONTIAC HIGHWAY HERALDS

The Pontiac Highway Heralds was a Bible Study and Prayer Club, which I gratefully helped start in 1934 at PHS along with Harold Souther, Chuck Wiser, Jim Savage, Mary Louise Stout, Marvel Kohen, Virginia Stapleton, and Marion Owens. Behind the scenes assisting us were Dr. Henry Savage, pastor of First Baptist Church, Mr. John Thor, Jr., principal of PHS, and Mr. Ralph Pardee, layman from First Baptist Church. We met each Friday afternoon, just after the last period, to sing, pray and have a short devotional. Later, we were able to meet in the morning, which was more helpful in starting the day on an inspirational tone. As our attendance grew, we moved to a larger meeting place arranged by Mr. Thor.

A CALL TO CHRISTIAN SERVICE

During the summer between high school and college, I went on a church retreat at Walled Lake State Park for all incoming college freshmen. It was Dr. Savage's last chance to challenge us to full time service for Christ. He made it clear that all of us are not called to full-time Christian service – some are called to be faithful in business, industry, education or some other field of work. Dr. Savage went on to say, "I believe God has already been leading many of you to full-time work for the Lord as preachers, missionaries, or church musicians." (In 1935 very few churches had full-time workers in categories other than those mentioned above.) After a challenging Bible lesson Dr. Savage asked, "How many of you feel that God is calling you to some area of Christian service?"

I was one of the first of the more than fifty young people who raised their hands in response. I had completely surrendered my life to God and felt He had been preparing me for this moment, but I had kept it a secret. I didn't know exactly what God wanted me to do, as I really felt an interest in doing all things. From the training with Dr. Pardee, I began to have a vision of missionary work. From Billy Souther, I learned I could have a career in music and education.

Dr. Savage urged all of us who made a surrender to come forward at invitation time on Sunday morning. He said, "This is a great personal victory for you, and you need to share this with our congregation. They will want to rejoice with you." I was very anxious for my dad to go to church with me that Sunday morning. When I told him I was going to be a minister, I thought he would be very pleased. To the contrary, he became upset. He said, "You can't even get up in a class and recite a poem without coming to tears." He was right. I would break out in a sweat and tears would come to my eyes. Eventually, I had to sit down.

My English teacher, Mrs. Rubert, was so considerate of my fear and me. She realized I was very shy and needed some encouragement. She only asked me questions that would require a yes or no answer. My dad didn't understand that I could outgrow my shyness with God's strength. During my first year in college, it seemed to look like my dad was right.

BILLY SOUTHER ESCORTS HAROLD AND ME TO OKLAHOMA BAPTIST UNIVERSITY

A few weeks before we left for Oklahoma Baptist University (OBU), Harold's brother took us for a visit to the campus. His wife Mildred was with him, and they wanted to go to Niagara Falls first. They said we had plenty of time, so to Niagara we went. It was a beautiful and awesome sight.

On the trip Billy gave lots of advice related to OBU. He told us that we should take every opportunity we could to study the leadership courses from the Sunday School Board. He assured us these courses would give us a thorough understanding of Southern Baptist work and practical training for Sunday

School and Baptist Young Peoples Union (BYPU). I had never heard of BYPU. Billy explained, "It's something like Christian Endeavor, but ten times better."

Billy also said that we needed to find a strong church with well-developed education and music programs. He suggested Immanuel Baptist Church where Dr. Tom Wiles was the pastor. He said, "Don't let them push you into a place of responsibility the first year. Take your time to get acquainted with how Southern Baptists operate, and it will be well worthwhile."

He added, "Just be a member of a class in Sunday School and a member of BYPU. Learn the parts that BYPU assigns weekly, but don't take your quarterly and read from it on Sunday evening when you meet. This will break you in on something you will constantly be called on to do in your career." Billy closed his advice-giving session by saying. "What I have told you today may have more to do with what you do for the Lord, regardless what that may be, than all the university and seminary may do for you."

A Drastic Change Of Plans

When we returned from our visit to the campus, Harold's mother had taken ill, so he couldn't go to school – at least until the next year. Someone needed to care for his mother because his papa was working full time at Pontiac Motors. This placed me in a dilemma. I didn't want to go to OBU by myself. I didn't know anyone there. My friends and pastor Dr. Savage began praying for me to know God's will. Some of my friends were going to Wheaton and others to Bob Jones College. I asked God to reveal His will. God answered our prayers, by closing the door at Wheaton because it was too late to register. Then, He opened the door at Bob Jones College.

I called the registrar's office at Bob Jones to see if there was a chance to enroll for the fall semester. They told me it was unusual to accept someone at such a late date (one week before school was to began), but for me to bring them my high school transcript and along with a letter of recommendation from Dr. Savage at First Baptist Church.

They also told me approximately how much money I would need up front and that I could arrange to pay the other fees on a monthly basis. I inquired about a work scholarship, and found out that I could probably get a part-time job with the National Youth Administration (NYA), which was a government program to help young people go to college during the depression years. The registrar said she would file my application for this.

After talking with the registrar, I went to my high school to get my transcript. The lady in the office told me they didn't give transcripts to former students but they would mail them at my request to any college or possible employer. I explained that I was going to Bob Jones the next week and the registrar had asked me to bring a transcript with me. She said, "We will mail it today, and it will be there before you get there." I asked her to examine my transcript and give me her opinion if I would be accepted or not. She looked it over and said, "You have a grade point average of 3.1 and I think that would be a shew in." I asked, "Are you sure you have the right transcript?" She replied, "Was your address 28 Euclid Ave?" "I answered, "I have lived there since I was a baby, and still live there." She quickly came back, "This is your transcript."

Wow! I was so relieved. Next, I went to First Baptist Church to see Dr. Savage. He greeted me warmly and told me he had been praying about my future. I thanked him for his prayers and told him God had led me to Bob Jones College. He was so happy and I was about to discovery why. He was on the Board of Trustees at Bob Jones College! I told him that they wanted a letter of recommendation from him, and he said, "I'll do more than that. I'll call Dr. Jones right now." And he did! I was so amazed and pleased that he said nice things about me.

When he finished talking to Dr. Jones, he asked me if I needed any help for college. I told him I could use any help I could get. He told me the church had a scholarship fund and he would tell the committee about me. That visit to Dr. Savage was a very profitable meeting. I received my letter, I was blessed by his phone call to Dr. Jones, and I encouraged by his kind words. Later, I received a nice check from the scholarship committee of the church.

Everything was coming together. I learned I qualified for a job with the NYA. And my dad was so supportive of me. When I left the following week he gave me a check for the money I needed up front. He also promised to send me a check each month for my room and meals. I had enough money saved to take care of my bus fare and my books and incidentals. I told my dad that I probably could make it without his monthly check because of my NYA job even though I didn't have the slightest idea what the job would pay. We decided he would pay for the first two months of room and board. (At the end of the first month I felt I could make it on my own, with few possible exceptions.)

On the Sunday before I left, the Highway Heralds Brass Quartet played for the morning service at First Baptist. Dr. Savage recognized all the young people who were going to college for the first time. Three were going to Bob Jones College: Janice Pardee, Marion Owens, and me. Another person planned to go, but decided to go to junior college instead.

The next day we left on a bus for Cleveland, Tennessee. We had fun on that long bus ride. Janice Pardee was so funny; she kept the whole bus in an uproar. Marion Owen was a little more dignified and reserved. She probably was ashamed of her loudmouth companions. I began to wonder if Bob Jones was ready for the likes of us. The closer we came to Cleveland, though I began to wonder if we were ready for Bob Jones! We didn't know what to expect. None of us had any idea of what the campus or atmosphere was like, but we were going to find out! I had reached another stage of my life. I was soon to be a college freshman.

BOB JONES COLLEGE, HERE I COME

When we arrived at Bob Jones College we were greeted like royalty. Some young men took our luggage and headed for the dorms, while we went to the registrar's desk. My first observation of the campus was that it was composed of a two-story brick building, which had been a residence, but now served as a classroom/office building. There were three dorm buildings, which appeared to be Army barracks but upgraded with brick siding. An auditorium was used for chapel and concerts. The office was nicely furnished with appropriate furniture that gave it a cheerful and home-like atmosphere. Behind the registrar's desk were two nicely framed pictures of Dr. Bob Jones, Sr. and Dr. Bob Jones, Jr.

After completing the registration forms, we were given a packet of materials, which included rules and regulations, directions to various locations on campus, and schedules for registration. We were then taken to our dormitories and introduced to the person in charge. There were five dormitory buildings: College Men, College Women, Academy Men, Academy Women, and one for Senior College Students, which had a section for men and a section for women.

These accommodations provided room and bath for two students. The other dorm rooms provided for four students with two bunk beds, study coves, and washbasins. Large toilet and shower facilities were at both ends of the hall. A senior student served as a monitor in each dorm, and he or she had a private room and bath.

All over the buildings and on every mirror in the dorms were signs, which read: Bob Jones College Is A Corporation Not For Profit. No Griping Tolerated! These signs and the lack of privacy offended me. I wondered what the girls thought. I knew how Janice would feel. She would make a big joke of it all. Marion would probably take it in stride and have no opinion at all, unless influenced by Janice. After calming down I decided to go with the flow. I figured God had led me here, and I would live by the rules and like it. Since I took care of myself most of the time after my mother died, I probably needed the discipline of group living. Plus, I would learn more from this by conforming than by having an ugly and uncooperative spirit.

My roommate was Randolph Maxwell, a fine young man from Atmore, Alabama. We really enjoyed our year together. In the room next to me was T. W. Wilson (who roomed with Billy Graham the year before and later became his assistant). Across the hall was Grady Wilson (who also became a part of the original Billy Graham team). They both left Bob Jones in the middle of the year. Neither expressed to anyone why they were leaving. Billy Graham attended Bob Jones only one semester. He then transferred to Florida Bible Institute located in Tampa. This was years before the Billy Graham Evangelistic Association was formed.

My job with NYA worked out great. I helped in an after-school program at a grade school in Cleveland, Tennessee. We took care of children until the parents came around five or six o'clock in the evening.

I found some excellent teachers at Bob Jones. They were all true to the Word and devoted Christians. Dr. Bob, as he was frequently called, was a great "home-spun" philosopher. His chapel messages were classics. I don't doubt his sincerity, and am not critical of his motives. He had a great ministry. Since I was there, Bob Jones College has grown to be one of the largest Christian universities and is now located in Greenville, North Carolina.

I played my trumpet for Chapel services twice and once for Sunday afternoon Vespers. The Vespers gave a classical platform for various artists among the faculty, and some from the student body. They attracted large crowds every Sunday afternoon and often featured Bob Jones, Jr., who was a very talented Thespian. He specialized in Shakespearean monologues.

OPPORTUNITIES TO PREACH

I also joined the Ministerial Association. They met twice a month for fellowship and one of the students would present a "short" (though rarely short) sermon. It was my privilege to have one of these assignments. I determined my message would be short. I had one of my friends to sit near the front to signal me a minute before my fifteen minutes would expire. To their amazement, and mine as well, I closed right on time.

The next week, I was pleased to be asked by the president of the Alliance if I would preach in some churches around Cleveland. He told me he needed someone to preach the following week at Ocoee Baptist Church. I asked where this was located and he told me it was twelve miles southeast at the intersection of Highway 40 and US 411. I asked how I would get there and he replied, "You have three options – find a friend who has a car, take a bus on Saturday afternoon, or hitchhike." He also told me I would have no trouble on Sunday morning catching a ride. I chose the latter option.

I knew I needed to leave early, so I left the school at six o'clock in the morning for the eleven o'clock service. Unfortunately, not a single car drove by in either direction that morning, so I walked all the way. I arrived just in time to step into the pulpit and preach. I repeated the sermon I gave for the Ministerial Association. I rehearsed it on that long walk.

After the service a gentleman, who appeared to be old enough to be my grandfather, approached me and asked if I knew Carson Hardy. He was his grandson and a student at Bob Jones. I knew him because he was in the William Jennings Bryan Society with me. This nice gentleman invited me for lunch in his home and told me he would drive me back to the college after the evening service. That was like music to my ears. He talked all afternoon, and I think I slept through some of his discourse, but it didn't seem to bother him. I was grateful for the meal, and especially the ride back. As I got out of his car, he handed me a five-dollar bill and thanked me for preaching. He said, "That was a good sermon."

THE DECISION TO STAY OR GO

Near the end of the year, the faculty gave each student a card to indicate if he or she planned on returning the next year. I filled out the card and indicated I didn't intend to return. Several days passed, and I was asked to report to the President's office. I had no idea what was about to occur.

He welcomed me to his office and asked me to be seated. He said, "I note by this card that you are not planning to be with us next year." I told him that was correct and explained my plans to go to Bob Jones for one year, then go to Oklahoma Baptist University with a boy who had led me to Christ. He asked how I liked Bob Jones and I felt I should tell the truth. I told him I hadn't been very happy with the school because of the legalism and harsh discipline. His countenance changed and he told me, "If anyone isn't happy at Bob Jones there must be something amiss in his spiritual life." This puzzled me for years until I heard that Billy Graham had a very similar experience with Dr. Jones.

I mention these two incidents to make this point. We need to be careful about judging others – someone could be severely wounded by our tongue. By God's grace, I was able to find encouragement and strength to put these things behind me and move toward the future God had planned. When, the year at Bob Jones ended, I headed home for a summer of work and play. I was approaching what proved to be some exciting days at OBU.

CHAPTER FIVE

THE SUMMER OF 1936

I had some happy experiences the summer of 1936. I attended two family reunions and visited with my brothers, cousins, aunts, and uncles. Best of all, my brother Carroll took Dad and me to two Detroit Tigers games. I have some great memories to look back on with my dad that summer.

My friend Harold Souther had a change of plans concerning college in the fall. His papa had now retired from Pontiac Motors and was taking care of Mom Souther. Harold was now the primary breadwinner – working at the Pontiac Motors plant full-time. He couldn't go to Oklahoma for another year. His family did everything they could to make enough money so Harold could go to OBU the next year. Fortunately, another boy named Cecil Hyatt from Pontiac was going to OBU. This allayed my fears of being alone so far away from home.

During the summer, the brass quartet enjoyed playing for several services at the First Baptist Church. Mr. Pardee asked us to do some mission work, but we couldn't because of our summer jobs. I worked part-time again at the Huntoon Funeral Home, where I had worked during my last year of high school.

In the fall, Billy Souther and his wife Mildred came to visit and take me to OBU. Billy had graduated from Southwestern Baptist Theological Seminary and was now Minister of Education at the Tabernacle Baptist Church in Fort Worth, Texas. Mildred was the director of children's work. Ramsey Pollard was their pastor.

On the trip to Shawnee, Billy reminded me of the things he said on our trip to Niagara the previous year. He prepared me for the difference I would find at OBU compared with Bob Jones. He said, "You will find an entirely new spirit. OBU will have so much more to offer you in a happy environment and unique preparation for ministry within the structure of the Southern Baptist Convention." He went on, "You probably received nothing like that at Bob Jones." He was right! As a freshman I couldn't even attend the Baptist church in Cleveland unless an upperclassman, or a faculty member accompanied me. In fact, Dr. Jones often made light of the main line denominations, saying they were theological liberals.

BECOMING A FULL FLEDGED BISON

We arrived at Shawnee, Oklahoma on a Thursday in the mid-afternoon. Billy advised me not to stay in the dormitory because it was so expensive. He said I should rent a room near OBU at Mrs. Mulkey's boarding house where I could also eat my meals. Billy had boarded there when he was at OBU.

We drove around the campus, and it looked too good to be true. The grounds were breathtaking. You entered the campus on a circular drive they called the "oval," which contained four buildings: Shawnee Hall, Montgomery Hall, Women's Dormitory, and Memorial Hall. Just past the oval and west of Shawnee Hall were the Gymnasium and Men's Dormitory. Other small buildings were across the street from the oval. After touring the campus, we drove to Mrs. Mulkey's house to inquire about the room and meals. She said she didn't have a room, but would be happy to serve me two meals a day, five days a week for fifteen dollars per week. That sounded great to me.

GETTING STARTED AT OBU

Mrs. Mulkey told me about an elderly couple named Mr. and Mrs. Lambdin who might consider renting a room to me – their previous boarder had recently graduated. What an answer to prayer! I had been in Shawnee less than an hour, and I already had a place to stay and eat.

We unloaded my luggage and personal belongings at the Lambdins and headed for registration at the school. Billy went with me and introduced me to many of the people in administration and some of the faculty. We learned that Dr. Fred Watts would be my Faculty Advisor. Billy and Mildred had been in his classes and were very close friends. After introducing me to Dr. Watts they left me in his care and left for their home in Fort Worth.

The Lord used Billy Souther to get me to OBU and to help me get situated in pleasant surroundings with such godly people. I lived with the Lambdins until I graduated from OBU three years later. They treated me like one of the family. They invited me to be with them for their family devotions each day, when my schedule at school would permit. Mr. Lambdin was also the brother of Dr. Jerry Lambdin, who was director of BYPU for the Southern Baptist Convention. I didn't know Dr. Lambdin then, but in later years, we became close friends. He gave me opportunities to lead conferences and direct music for Baptist Training Union weeks at Ridgecrest.

I never for one moment felt like a stranger at OBU. From the president and his wife to the faculty and my fellow students, I had the assurance that I had found God's place for me. The only thing I missed was Harold Souther. Although he wasn't there, I knew that this was God's plan. I really yearned for the day when he would join me and I prayed that he would be my roommate at the Lambdins.

God confirmed my decision about eating my meals with the Mulkeys. They had two sons who were musicians and singers in the vocal music department of OBU. We got acquainted at supper, which was always delicious and plentiful. Mrs. Mulkey was an excellent cook and served home-cooked food with fresh vegetables, delectable desserts, and the best hot rolls I ever tasted. After my first supper with them, the Mulkey brothers asked me to join them in trying out for the University Male Quartet. I said, "I can't sing. I play the trumpet." They said, "Come on anyway. It will be a fun evening even if you don't get in the quartet." I didn't have anything better to do, so I trailed along.

SING OR NOT TO SING, THAT WAS THE QUESTION!

About fifteen guys, including me met to audition for two vacancies in the quartet – a second tenor and a baritone. I didn't have the slightest hope of being chosen, nor was I sure I wanted to be chosen. I met the lady in charge: Dr. Ruth Mitchell (she later married George Roesch, a Shawnee Funeral Director). She led the group through some vocal exercises, then asked each of us to sing a song of our own selection. I had no idea what to sing. Morris Mulkey said,

"Sing 'The Old Rugged Cross.' Surely you know it." Dr. Mitchell told me politely, " Very nice," I noticed she said the same thing to each one trying out.

Next, Dr. Mitchell asked us to sing our respective part with two other quartet members: Forest Stith, first tenor and Raymond Hall, bass. I didn't have the slightest idea which part to sing. Several others said the same thing. So we tried both second tenor and baritone.

When we finished, Dr. Mitchell said she would post the names of the two winners on the bulletin board in Shawnee Hall by ten o'clock the next day. She then explained what was involved in being a member of the OBU Male Quartet. First, we had to take voice lessons and attend regular practice sessions twice a week. We also had to be available to travel every weekend when needed. She then told us about the importance of the quartet to the university.

She explained that the male quartet was an important arm of outreach for the university. They gave several weekend concerts at high schools, and after the concerts they met with the students to tell them about OBU. They also showed a movie about the school and distributed materials. In exchange for this service, the members received an honorarium from the offering taken at each appearance. The offering was divided by five, with each singer receiving twenty percent, and the university receiving the remaining twenty percent to cover expenses. OBU furnished the car, driver and manager.

To Sing In The Quartet Or Not

Dr. Mitchell closed the audition by saying, "I need to know tonight whether you will join, if selected." I didn't know how to respond to Dr. Mitchell. I had already registered for my classes and my schedule would have to change so I could take the voice lessons. I explained my dilemma to her and she told me she wanted me! I couldn't believe it since some of the others had better voices than me. She explained that my voice had a quality that would easily blend with the other three voices. She also complimented my musicianship. "You read music well and that is very important," she said. "I will not require a decision from you tonight. You take time to pray about your decision. Call Billy

Souther and get his opinion. Just let me know by next Monday morning." In addition, she said, "I will hold the place for you for a week."

I appreciated the fact that she would hold the quartet position for me, and that she asked me to pray about it. I believe she was trying to teach me a spiritual lesson about the need of prayer in every decision of life. I did pray about it, and sought prayer support from Harold and Billy Souther, and my pastor from home. Billy Souther told me how much his quartet experiences had meant to him and his ministry. I talked to Dr. Savage in Pontiac and he also encouraged me to take the place in the quartet.

The only thing left was to ask Dr. Watts if it was too late to change my schedule. He said it wouldn't be a problem, but I would need to decide which class to drop from my elective list. The only choice possible was to give up band! What a life-changing decision that would be! I had been in instrumental music since junior high school. I had never been in vocal music. I knew I probably wouldn't keep up the trumpet if I were not in the band.

From all the encouragement I received from trusted and experienced friends, I felt the moving of God's peace in my heart to give up band and pursue voice. I answered His call as He was fulfilling His promise of Jeremiah 29:11. You see! "He had plans for me, my life, my hope and my future." I stepped into unchartered territory knowing God was in charge.

Almost immediately God confirmed His calling by opening up other opportunities. In addition to singing in the Male Quartet, I was given another NYA job. This time, I wasn't babysitting children after school, I was coaching the University Mixed Quartet!

During my years at OBU I garnered two leading roles in the operas, "Martha" and "The Bohemian Girl." In my junior year, I sang the role of the prophet Elijah from the oratorio by the same name and in my senior year, I sang the bass solo parts in "The Messiah."

THE FALL SEMESTER OF 1936

I can't begin to tell you what the OBU Male Quartet meant to me. We had such exciting experiences and met almost two hundred pastors in our concert tours each year. We also sang at the Oklahoma Baptist State conventions, annual association meetings, and at the Ridgecrest and Falls Church Conference Centers. All of this drew me out of my shell and gave a boost to my self-image. This was God at work. At the time, I didn't realize it, but in retrospect I am amazed how God gave me the strength to do all of these seemingly impossible tasks.

On my third voice lesson with Dr. Mitchell, she told me her plans to produce the opera "The Bohemian Girl" the following year. This would be the first opera ever produced at OBU. She then threw out a challenge, which nearly threw me off my feet. She said, "Elmer, I want you to sing the male lead." I didn't feel I was ready for this, so I said, "Dr. Mitchell, I think this is way over my head, and besides, I am not in the School of Fine Arts and some of the upper class students will be expecting such a role." She scolded me and said, "I am the director of the Fine Arts School and I will choose the best suited. I know your potential, trust me."

Then, she told me the production was set for April 1937 – only eight months away! How could I possibly learn all the words and music, keep up my grades and maintain the heavy schedule of the Male Quartet? Humanly speaking it was impossible.

I shared this with her and she quoted Matthew 19:26b: "With men this is impossible; but with God all things are possible." Though, she took this verse out of context, she made her point!

The rest of the year was a whirlwind. Most of my time was spent rehearsing for the opera, singing with the quartet, and serving with the Ministerial Alliance and the Kalalians. OBU had six social societies designed for fellowship, intramural sports, and charitable ministries. I joined the Kalalians and just before the year ended, I was honored and privileged to be elected president. If there was one activity that took the most time, it was the opera "The Bohemian Girl." It was a tremendous project.

James Sapp, who was Manager of the OBU Male Quartet for several years, was responsible for taking care of all the details. For instance, he had to get a specific waiver so we could use our own sound technicians, lighting technicians, and backstage people. He also rented our costumes from the Metropolitan Opera in New York. Hours of rehearsing from September to April culminated in two outstanding performances on Friday evening, April 9, 1937, and again on Monday evening, April 12, 1937. When all was said and done, Dr. Mitchell, Mr. Sapp, the production crew, chorus, performers, and orchestra members were exhausted, but thrilled.

The Shawnee Press carried this headline on Tuesday, April 13: "OBU OPERA PRODUCTION HAILED AS GREAT." The story continued, "Color from the stage door to the back row of the gallery characterized the Oklahoma Baptist University Fine Arts School's presentation of Balfe's 'The Bohemian Girl' last Friday and Monday nights. Profuse costumes and hue-full stage settings greeted the eyes of more than 5,000 patrons of the finer arts who left the hall after the performance saying the opera was a great success. Dr. J. W. Raley, president of OBU, when reached immediately after the last curtain said, 'This is the finest thing for cultural development since I have been here. It's the way we want to go.' "

So it went – with congratulations all around. We all enjoyed the work and time that was involved in the opera. However, I believe we were all glad when it was over. Now, it was back to the books and we had to cram. Final exams would hit us in the next few weeks.

What did all this effort and time have to do with this story? Well, I am a firm believer that God is involved in my life. I never want to get out of His will, or outside the plans that He has for me. I believe the opera was a blessing to me in several ways. First, Mr. Sapp and Dr. Mitchell loved God and their influence contributed to my spiritual growth. They prayed with me and helped me find my way. Second, the discipline, which the opera required of me in learning the music and memorizing my lines, was a blessing to me. Third, the camaraderie with the Christian young people in working and praying together was an encouragement to me. That God would use the opera to expand our knowledge and to use this knowledge to help us present the Gospel was an awesome revelation to me. I wouldn't have dreamed that my opera experiences at OBU would prepare me for the work I would do in churches twenty to thirty years later.

SUMMER OF 1937

When school was out for the summer, I hitchhiked home and applied for a summer job at the GMC plant in Pontiac. They hired me on the spot for the eleven to seven shift, and I began work the next night. I had never worked a night shift before, and it was difficult to change my sleeping habits. By the time I had to go back to OBU, I was just getting adjusted. The GMC plant manufactured and assembled buses. My job was to operate a stamping machine, which punched holes on metal panels. It wasn't a hard job, but it was boring (no pun intended).

I got the knack of it quickly and began increasing my speed. A Union man came over to me and with words I didn't use, he asked me why I was in such a big hurry. Evidently I was turning out more panels per hour than the Union allowed. He said. "Relax, take it easy, you're going twice as fast as GMC expects." Seeing that he was a big muscular man, I decided to slow down!

During our breaks, I was able to witness. A few of the fellows started calling me "preacher." I took it in stride and even felt it was a compliment. Some Christian men asked me to read the Bible and pray for them. I gladly accepted the invitation.

My dad was very busy that summer, but we were still able to share several evening meals together and even bowl a few times. We also visited with my brothers and their families, as well as uncles, aunts, and cousins – most on my mother's side. All that was left of the Bailey clan was my dad, his two brothers, their four daughters and yours truly. My Grandfather Bailey had two sons, and my Great Grandfather Bailey had only one son, Harmon. I began to wonder how we could keep the Bailey name going for another generation. Later on you will see how God took care of the problem.

Things had worked out well for Harold's folks and he was able, along with his dad's help, to save enough money to enroll at OBU. We just knew things would open up for him as they did for me.

The summer offered us opportunities to sing or play our trumpets. I hadn't played very much for two years, so it was difficult for me. Now, Harold had really improved since high school, as he practiced every day. He had become quite an artist. He continued using the trumpet as a platform for giving his testimony. In a way I envied him, but God had led me in another musical direction, developing my vocal skills. God has plans for each of us and it is up to us to find God's will and way.

Harold and I discussed how we would travel to Oklahoma. We didn't have much of a choice – it was either walk, hitchhike, ride the bus, or fly. We decided to pray first, then make that decision as we approached the end of the summer.

It was during the summer, that I realized Harold's father and mother had never met my dad. I talked to Dad about this and asked if he would like to meet the Southers. He hesitated before he said, "I am not sure. Please don't take me wrong, but you know I am a very shy man." I teased him a little about being really shy around people he didn't know. If he knew you, he was not shy at all. For instance, he was outgoing around the Spanish American War veterans and his Masonic Lodge buddies. In fact, he was very active in leadership of these organizations. Maybe, he felt these Christian people would try to push their Christianity on him. He never said anything like that. It was just my opinion. Eventually, he said, "I will think about it." But, it didn't happen.

Harold and I also had many opportunities to visit our home church that summer. It was surprising to see how the makeup of the congregation had changed so quickly. Some of the staff members had moved on to other places. Several of our close friends had gone off to college, while others had left for mission projects, as we had done during previous summer months.

Dr. Savage and his wife were attentive to Harold and me – even though their boys, Jim and Bob, were away for the summer. The Savages included Harold and me in all the functions at their home just like they did when we were in high school. I am sure this filled a void in their "empty nest."

By the end of the summer, Harold told me he planned to take the bus to Shawnee because he had a lot of luggage, plus a large suitcase and a steamer trunk. Hitchhiking was not a practical alternative. He decided to leave before me in order to register and settle in at the Lambdins before school started.

I decided to wait and go to OBU the following week, so I could earn another forty dollars from my job. A few days after Harold left, Dad called and asked me to have supper with him. He told me he had a surprise for me. I had no idea what the surprise was and thought this might be my last chance to be with him before going back to OBU. He said he would pick me up at home at 5:30. I didn't have to be at work until 11 p.m., so that gave us plenty of time together, plus time to change to work clothes and get to work on time.

We had a nice supper at a buffet diner. He didn't say a word about the surprise. Instead, he asked questions about the subjects I would be taking in the coming year. I told him about Balfe's "The Bohemian Girl" opera, which we presented in April, and that it was the first opera ever produced by the university. I proudly reported that I had the male lead. He scolded me for not telling him sooner and said, "I would have enjoyed seeing it. I am proud of you. This school has done a lot for you." We also talked about what his plans were going to be while I was away at school.

After we finished eating he pulled out an envelope from his coat pocket and said, "This is an early Christmas present." My anxiety had almost peaked. When I opened the envelope there were some papers enclosed and I noticed my name at the top of what was the title to a car. It was Dad's 1936 Ford, which he purchased the year those cars first hit the market. Talk about surprise! I was bowled over! I jumped up and hugged my dad and thanked him over and over, right in the diner before God and everybody. He put the keys in my hand and said, "I don't want you to hitchhike any more!"

This gift topped the gift of my first electric train; the excitement surpassed my moving from knickers to long pants during my first years at high school. It was time for a celebration! Then I thought about Harold. If he hadn't been in such a hurry we could have ridden together. I understood; I remembered how anxious I was to get to OBU my first year. I decided to surprise Harold when I arrived.

How Did My Room Get So Small?

When I arrived at the Lambdins, Harold wasn't there. Mrs. Lambdin said he was buying books at the bookstore. With little more than a greeting, I jumped in my car and drove to the bookstore. He was right where Mrs. Lambdin said he would be and he was ready to leave the bookstore with a supply of books and school supplies – more than one person could carry.

As soon as he saw me, he rushed to greet me with a hug and said, "Boy, you have arrived at just the right time to help me get these books to our room." I said, "Wait a minute, freshman. I am not your servant, but I will take you and all your supplies in my car!" With a look of bewilderment, he said, "What car?" I picked up some of his books and said, "Grab the rest of your stuff and follow me." When we got to the car I proudly announced, "This is my car!" Well, to say he was surprised would be putting it mildly. Then as I drove to the Lambdins, I explained the whole story of how Dad and I had gone to dinner, and he had surprised me with the title to the car.

We drove back to our room at the Lambdins and rearranged things to give us more room. Then, we filled the trunk of the car with our empty suitcases and other things we wouldn't use on a daily basis.

It was about suppertime, so I asked him what he was doing. He said, "No plans." I replied, "Let's call Mrs. Mulkey and see if she can take us. This is our celebration night. We have finally become roommates. I'm so glad you're here, and I'm so thankful I have this car. Isn't God good?" Mrs. Mulkey welcomed me back and told me to bring Harold on over – she had plenty. It was a happy reunion with Harold and the Mulkey crowd.

We visited with Mr. and Mrs. Lambdin when we returned. They wanted to know what we did all summer. They also invited us to have breakfast with them the next morning. Harold and I had our prayer time after breakfast, then headed over to the campus. I needed to register and talk with my faculty adviser about my schedule. Harold told me that Ruth Mitchell asked about me and wanted to see me as soon as I arrived. So, I headed for her office in Montgomery Hall – the home base of the Fine Arts School.

Dr. Mitchell greeted me with a friendly hug and asked about my summer. She said, "Elmer, I have exciting news about our music program. Our Annual Christmas Music Festival will be broadcast over the Oklahoma Mutual Network. I have selected a very beautiful cantata, 'The Light Eternal,' and I want you to sing the baritone solo. In addition, we will sing this cantata in Raley Chapel for the student body. If you have a minute, I'd like you to listen to the solo, then sight-read the vocal part as I play the piano. I know you are going to love it."

She moved to the piano and played a very unusual rendition of "While Shepherds Watched Their Flocks By Night." After hearing it only once, I attempted to sing it through as she played. I was so encouraged when she said, "I am thrilled how your voice has matured in just one year. Your solo in 'Elijah' this year was magnificent, and your contribution to 'The Bohemian Girl' was superb." I told her it was because she allowed God to use her skills and knowledge to help me develop the talent God had given me.

Dr. Mitchell then showed me a scrapbook, which contained news clippings and more for all the music programs she directed. There were some articles and pictures from The Shawnee News that I hadn't seen. The journalist who reviewed "The Bohemian Girl" gave a vividly glowing report. Let me refer to a few lines from this article: "The writer was impressed not only with the music, but the scenery and the complicated logistics involved in producing an opera – the legal responsibility of complying with copyright laws, obtaining copyrights for music and orchestrations, rental of the Civic Auditorium in Shawnee." And he was right!

GOD DELIVERS A WARNING BLOW

Before my sophomore year had gotten into full swing, Dean Solomon summoned me to his office. He expressed his concern for my academic standing, "How do you explain your grades for the last semester as compared with your first semester?" I told him I was aware that my grades had suffered recently, but I wasn't sure why. He then asked me to enumerate my extracurricular tasks – president of the Kalalians, singer in the opera, coach of the Mixed Quartet, member of the Male Quartet, and the Ministerial Alliance, and . . ." Before I could finish, he interrupted, "I think we both know your problem, don't we?"

He complimented me for being involved in so many activities of campus life at the university, then he told me to make a list of the activities in which I was involved. Next, he said to assign a priority number to each item, then chop off the lowest priorities. He said, "You may find some items are taking more time than others. Use good judgment in making these decisions. I believe it is of top priority that you have sufficient time to study and prepare for the classes you are taking." He concluded by praying for me. He thanked God for my zeal and the talents He had given me, then he asked God to give me vision and wisdom in working through this problem.

I believe God used Dean Solomon to wake me up to reality. In my enthusiasm to get involved, I became inefficient in what should have meant the most. He gave me a lesson on priorities. I wonder how many universities have men who care enough to help.

It appeared difficult at first to drop some of my activities, but after I assigned the priorities, I knew what I had to do. You will never guess the first thing I eliminated because it was probably the thing I enjoyed the most. I had been on the OBU Male Quartet for almost two years and it was the most time-consuming of my activities.

I talked with Dr. Mitchell and asked to be relieved of my quartet positions as singer and coach. But, I also told her that I would still sing with the opera "Martha" and keep my assignment in the Christmas Cantata. I couldn't let Dr. Mitchell down after all she had done for me. Before I left, I offered her some suggestions for two positions on the Male Quartet – Bill Thompson as baritone and Bill Reynolds as bass. I added that my friend Harold Souther was well qualified to serve as coach for the Mixed Quartet. Next, I asked the Kalalian Social Club if I could be relieved as president. Only a few months remained in my term of office anyway.

I thoroughly enjoyed all of these activities but the increase of my grade average from a "C" to an "A" by the end of the school year was worth it all. When I brought my report card to Dean Solomon, I thanked him for all his advice, "Dean, you probably taught the best lesson of my university days that afternoon in your office. I can see it will be profitable to me all my life."

THE BEGINNINGS OF THE BISON GLEE CLUB AT OBU

In the Spring of 1938 a dream of Dean Warren Angell became a reality with the founding of the Male Glee Club. Harold and I became two of the thirty-five men selected for charter membership. We were thrilled! We named the group

"Sangerbund," which was German for "singing group." When it became clear that World War II was eminent, we quickly changed the name to the Bison Glee Club.

This group, directed by Dean Angell until he retired, has an amazing record of achievements. It is recognized as one of finest music groups of its kind – even beyond Southern Baptist circles. I count it a privilege to have been one of the founding members and cherish the experiences we had.

There have been many reunions of the Bison Glee Club through the years, but two have a special place in my heart: Dean Angell's 90th Birthday in 1997 and the Bison Glee Club's 60th Anniversary in 1998. The Dean's birthday was an exciting event for the large number of Glee Club Alumni in attendance. It was amazing to see his high level of energy and his ability at the keyboard was as keen as ever. It was also a thrilling experience once again to sing many of the Glee Club numbers under his direction. The 60th Anniversary was wonderful, as well. The current Glee Club serenaded us, and later we had the privilege to sing along with them on "Dry Bones" and Dean's superb composition, "OBU Alma Mater."

SUMMER OF 1938

Just before school was out for summer vacation I received a letter from Rev. J. C. Dodson, Pastor of Pike City Baptist Church in Fox, Oklahoma. He heard the OBU Male Quartet sing at the Oklahoma Baptist Convention in Oklahoma City and the Southern Baptist Convention in New Orleans. Then, he contacted the OBU to see if one of the singers might be available during the third week of June to conduct an evening revival and direct a morning Vacation Bible School. I guess the school recommend me.

In his letter, he gave me some facts and figures on his church and a brief introduction to himself and his family. He indicated the church would take care of my traveling expenses, lodging, meals, and even take a love offering for me. The church would also use the curriculum published by Southern Baptist Sunday School Board and train all the workers. I would be responsible for directing the opening period each morning as outlined in the material.

Rev. Dodson concluded his letter with his phone number and asked me to call him as soon as possible since the event was only six weeks away. This was the first such invitation I had ever received. In my eagerness to get to work for the Lord, I called him that very day after a short prayer. I know now that I should have prayed and studied all of this a little more, but in my naivete I called and told him I would love to accept his invitation.

I was very honest when I told him about my walk with the Lord. I was saved when I was in high school about six years earlier and had never preached a revival. In fact, I told him I had only preached about four or five times. I also said I had never directed a Vacation Bible School in my life except in Northern Michigan when I was a new Christian, and even then we had no workers, literature, or materials.

There was a brief pause, then he started to laugh. I didn't know whether to laugh or cry. He quickly alleviated my confusion by saying, "Oh, Brother Bailey, I didn't want you to preach, I wanted you to lead the music. I am sorry. I have a copy of my letter here and I wasn't clear what I wanted. I said I wanted you to conduct a revival, but let me reword that sentence. We want you period! We have an evangelist, Rev. Hamblin from First Baptist of Healdton, Oklahoma."

He also relieved my fears about Vacation Bible School. He told me, "We have had Vacation Bible School every year since we came here, and my wife has been principal. She knows VBS backward and forward. We need you to conduct the opening sessions as they are outlined in the material. Let the Lord direct and use you. If you do not know VBS now, you will be an expert when we get through."

J. C. Dodson endeared himself to my heart right then and there. He was altogether real – a sensitive and loving man with a fabulous sense of humor. And his church had the same realness about them, as well. What made these people so effervescent, loving, and capable? I found out from his preaching. He was full of the Spirit of God, and so was his wife.

What a wonderful week of spiritual renewal it was for me. Mrs. Dodson had VBS so organized. All the workers and the children were in the palm of her hand. I got more out of that week than I did in any course on education. It was also the revival I needed. I thank God for the several who found Jesus as Savior, and for others who recommitted their lives to Him.

On the afternoon of that last Sunday, J. C. Dodson said that he felt God was prompting him to ask me to be their summer music leader and help build the Sunday School. He said, "The oil fields here are full of young married people with lots of children, and plenty of middle-aged adults with teenagers. We must find them, reach them and win them to Jesus." He also said that if it worked out over the summer, he wanted me to consider doing this each weekend through the school year. He wanted to start a youth choir, and also encourage the ladies to start a children's choir. He added that if my schoolwork or activities conflicted, the church would excuse me – all they asked is that I give them at least, a 24-hours notice.

In return, he said the church would take care of my car expenses, provide lodging and meals, and pay me thirty dollars a week during the summer and twenty dollars per week during the school year. Rev. Dodson concluded his offer by saying, "If you feel the Lord leading you to do this and could give me an answer before church tonight. I would like to present this idea at the close of the service. If you need more time to think and pray about this, we will wait until you come to a definite decision before proceeding. We like your spirit, Elmer. We need someone just like you and we'll try to make this a learning experience for you. I'll support you in everything to which you and I have agreed. If we are not in agreement on something, we will talk it out by ourselves. I am open-minded and by no means stubborn. With God as our leader and our hearts in tune with Him, I believe we will make a great team. God will bless!"

Before the evening service, I told Rev. Dodson that I felt God's leading to accept his offer for the summer, but that I needed to wait until I got my class schedule before making a commitment beyond then. What a glorious service of praise and worship we experienced that night. Rev. Hamblin was excellent and his invitation was simple and clear, to which many responded!

After the service, Rev. Dodson recognized a committee to start the proceeding. They offered a motion that the church call me to work through the summer as music and education director at a salary of twenty-five dollars a week with lodging and meals provided by the members in a plan to be determined by the ladies of the church. The vote was unanimous and the church gave me a standing ovation. Before Rev. Hamblin (the revival evangelist) left he said, "I want to talk with you before I leave." I said, "Okay, but give me a few minutes to greet the folks." The people were so excited but no more than I. They were so gracious. The lady who entertained me in her home during the revival, Mrs. Ruth Phipps, came by to say she and her husband would be glad for me to stay with them for the summer. They owned the only store and gas station in Fox and lived in a large home nearby. During the revival, I stayed in their guest cabin in the back yard.

Remembering that Rev. Hamblin was waiting for me, I excused myself and we went into the pastor's office to talk. He congratulated me on the music during the revival and on my call to the church. Then, he asked me if I knew any other student at OBU who might be interested in a similar position. He needed someone to help him at his church in Healdton, Oklahoma. I told him about Harold Souther and how he helped me to find Christ when we were in high school. I gave him a brief bio about his musicianship, leadership skills, and involvement in the music program at the university.

I said, "I'm going back to Shawnee on Monday morning and can tell Harold if you are interested in talking with him. He isn't in school this summer and may come back with me on Tuesday. This would give you the opportunity for a personal interview and also a chance for him to lead music for Sunday services if he desired." He agreed, so I told him I would talk to Harold.

As I was getting ready to leave the church that night, Rev. Dodson came by and hugged my neck. He said, "I'm so glad you are going to work with me. I am going to be praying for you and your trip home and back. I shall also be praying that God will open the doors for you to remain with us after classes begin. Here is an envelope. It contains your share of our love offering for you and your travel expenses. If the expense reimbursement isn't sufficient, just let me know."

I thanked him and told him I planned to be back in the late afternoon on Tuesday. I said, "I want you to know that I fell in love with you during our first phone conversation. It was really funny, but at first I couldn't understand why you were laughing. After you explained, I laughed with you. I think that revealed the flexibility in both of us. I also am indeed grateful for the love offering. See you Tuesday night."

When I got back to the cabin that night, I called Harold. I told him what I knew and that he would need to go with me on Tuesday to talk with Rev. Hamblin if he was interested – and he was! I had made arrangements for him to stay with me at the Phipps through Sunday. Rev. Hamblin called before I left Monday and told me to bring Harold back on Tuesday, so he could lead music on Sunday. In the meantime they would have a chance to talk.

I arrived back in Shawnee around noon on Monday. Harold and I ate lunch, then we visited our faculty advisors to see if we could arrange our schedules so we would have no classes on Friday afternoon or Monday morning. They both said it was too early to make such a decision, but thought it could be arranged at registration time.

I shared our plans with Dr. Mitchell and assured her we would be available to rehearse for the opera and Christmas cantata. She was somewhat concerned about Harold's responsibilities on the Mixed Quartet. I told her that Harold hadn't talked with the Healdton pastor but would do so in a few days. Then, I explained that since I already had an understanding with the pastor in Fox about conflicts and the priority of OBU items that Harold would make similar arrangements with the pastor in Healdton. This seemed to ease her concerns, but I was sure she wasn't happy about it. I think she didn't want to give us up. When I left, she wished us well and said she knew this would be an invaluable experience for us.

The next morning, I packed heavy since I was going to be gone the rest of the summer. Harold packed heavy, as well, but his decision was not so certain. He would know before the week was over. We spent time praying on the way. (Of course, whoever was driving had to keep his eyes open and his hands on the wheel.)

Mrs. Phipps had the welcome sign out when we arrived. She said, "It's too late for lunch but we want you fellows to be our guests for supper tonight. I have asked Rev. Dodson and his wife to join us." I unpacked all my gear from the car, but Harold took out only what he would need through Sunday. We spent the afternoon looking around Fox. It didn't take long since it was a small town. We passed locations where they were drilling for oil. It was interesting to see the oil wells pumping. We went by Pike City Baptist Church and took a tour of the buildings. No one was around but the buildings were wide open (we weren't accustomed to this).

The next morning I took Harold over to Healdton, which was about twenty-five miles away. He had an appointment to see the pastor at ten o'clock. I left him at the church and decided to look around the town. It appeared to be the county seat and a little larger than Fox. On the main street, there were several stores, plus the Courthouse, which was the prominent structure in the downtown area. The First Baptist Church was made of brick and stone and had a steeple. The building appeared much more attractive and well kept than Pike City Baptist.

I walked around the downtown area and talked with some men on the street. One was a lawyer who told me he was a member of First Baptist Church. I introduced myself as an OBU student and that I would be working that summer with Pike City Baptist Church in Fox. He asked where I was from and I told him Pontiac, Michigan. He asked the same old question, "What brought you way out here for college?" I replied, "That's a long story."

Thinking Harold might be through with his interview, I returned to the church and found Harold and Pastor Hamblin in the Worship Center. Hamblin was first to speak as he said, "Well Brother Elmer, I want to introduce you to our new music director." Harold was giving his typical grin. They both seemed overjoyed, so I joined the celebration! The pastor thanked me for bringing Harold and told me that he was just the one he needed. Since it was lunchtime, he invited both of us to be his guest for lunch at the Healdton Cafe.

After lunch, Harold unloaded the rest of his things from the car. The lawyer I had spoken to earlier came by and the pastor introduced him. He announced that Harold would be staying with him and his family for the summer. Isn't it a small world? Well, Harold put his things back into my car, and we followed the lawyer to his house. This gave us an opportunity to talk about his interview. His arrangements with Hamblin were practically identical to that of the Pike City Church. I could tell that he had been talking with Brother Dodson. Even the financial arrangements were the same. Harold expressed his appreciation to me for my help. I told Harold, "I don't think I had much to do with it. The whole thing was God working out His plans for the both of us." Harold agreed and we sang "The Doxology."

When Harold was settled, I drove back to Fox, singing and praising God all the way. What a great summer we had! It is truly a miracle story. Both churches had choirs of similar size and were in dire need of help. Though they had excellent instrumentalists, the choir was not organized and had little choir music. What choir music they had, it was no challenge to the singers. Choir rehearsals were also poorly attended.

With much prayer and planning, we saw more and more people begin attending. We felt we were learning far more than the choirs. We also started youth choirs. Harold had far more youth than I had, but gradually our numbers grew every week. We started directing our choirs in unison, then we introduced two parts, and then three parts. Before summer was over we were able to do some four-part music.

We enlisted women to start the children's choirs. We helped them along in finding music for them to sing. We also trained the ladies to teach the children to sing and not to "holler." God blessed us and the people began to see the glorious part music plays in the life of the church.

The people were so responsive. They came to see themselves as the "praise leaders" of the congregation. But we cannot take all the credit. Most of the credit must go to the Lord. We were so green, but we loved the Lord and found joy and blessing in leading them along.

How time flew that summer! Before we knew it, the summer was over and we were back in Shawnee registering for the 1938-1939 school year.

ANOTHER ROMANTIC EXPERIENCE

It was the first day of the 1938-1939 school year, and sitting next to me in one of my classes was a new student. She was a very attractive girl and new at the university. I felt it my duty to make her welcome. I introduced myself and she told me her name was Fern Long from Eagle City, Oklahoma. She was a transfer student from Northwest Oklahoma Junior College and was classified as a freshman. A campus music concert was scheduled for Thursday night, so I asked if she would be my date. She was really glad to meet a new friend and accepted my invitation. We met in the parlor of the Memorial Dorm at 6:30 p.m.

She told me her folks were farmers and that she had an older brother and younger sister. They had three horses, lots of chickens, and four milk cows. I told her about my family and my background in Michigan. We had a great time, and went to see a movie on the following Thursday night. I discovered that she wasn't a Christian after our first date, so I asked her if we could talk about this when we got back to the dorm. She agreed and seemed pleased by my concern.

We found a quiet corner in the parlor, and I had the privilege of leading her to accept Christ as Savior. I asked if she had a Bible and she did not. I had an extra one, which I loaned her. I also had a Gospel tract entitled "Helps For New Christians" which I gave her. She evidently had no church background. I told her I would be glad to help her along in this new experience. I suggested that she join a church and explained what Baptists believe about baptism.

The very next Sunday Fern made a public profession of faith at University Baptist Church, and presented herself for baptism. She was baptized and joined Sunday School and BYPU the following Sunday. She was so happy and thanked me many times for my help. She was so eager to learn. I knew that if she could help lead someone to Christ, it would be an event the Holy Spirit would use to strengthen her. I told her what I thought and she said, "Elmer, if you will help me, I'll try!"

The Baptist Student Union office had a neat booklet on how to witness for Christ. I promised I would help her after she studied the booklet and memorized the Scriptures. My plan was to act as if I were not saved and ask her to use the Scripture to show me, first why I needed Christ, second how Jesus paid the price for my sin, and lastly that salvation is a gift of God and I can do nothing to earn my salvation. I tried to make it clear that we cannot win someone to Christ, only the Spirit of God can do that. Our role is to pray for the Holy Spirit to work in the one to whom we are witnessing, and the Spirit will give us the wisdom, power, and courage as we witness to that person.

I told Fern, "Let's find a time when you can rehearse with me the steps to take in witnessing to someone. Then, we'll pray that God will lead you to the one who will be waiting for your witness." We set a date for Thursday night. Before we left that session we prayed and agreed to be prayer partners. We made a list of people to include my dad and two brothers, plus Fern's parents, her brother and sister. Our schedules made it virtually impossible for us to pray together, so we shared our prayer lists and had our quiet times separately.

Harold and I continued our weekend ministries – I was so thankful for the car Dad gave me in 1937. Without some type of transportation, it would have been impossible for us to get to Fox and Healdton. Since we were rooming and eating off campus, the car became more than a convenience, it was a necessity.

When I got back from one of my weekend trips, I told Fern, "Let's find a time when we can drive to Eagle City so I can meet your folks." She thought that spring break would be a good time. Fern asked her folks and cleared our plans with the Dean of Women. We decided to leave Monday afternoon and return on Friday. That way, Harold and I wouldn't miss a Sunday with our churches.

We had a good time "down on the farm." I wasn't prepared for its size. I don't know how many acres they had, but you could see their property for miles in every direction. It was beautiful to behold – like you were looking at a sea of gold. Sometimes, when a breeze was blowing it appeared as golden waves of grain, ready for the harvesting time. Fern's folks seemed to be happy, humble, and hard-working people. I also enjoyed Fern's little sister; she was the life of the party. They invited me to visit again.

When we returned to school, we needed to cram for mid-term exams. We hadn't cracked a book the whole week we were in Eagle City.

MY OPPORTUNITY WITH THE OPERA "MARTHA"

The rest of the spring flew by and summer came and went. It was the fall before I knew it and Dr. Mitchell (my voice teacher) was sharing with me a plan to produce another opera in the spring of 1939. She then threw out a challenge, which almost took me off my feet. She said, "I want you to sing a support role in the opera by Flotow, called 'Martha.' "

Just as she did the time before, she went to the piano and played a few bars of the amusing aria of Sir Tristram Mickleford. She twisted my arm and I agreed to try it. This would be my last "hurrah" in the opera business, as I would graduate the day after the production. Wayne Taylor had the tenor lead and was magnificent in the theme aria, which is probably one of the most familiar of operatic arias. Nancy Montgomery, singing in the role of Martha, was superb in her part as she was in the 1937 production of "The Bohemian Girl."

AN EVENT THAT COULD HAVE BEEN TRAGIC

I cannot leave OBU days without relating a story that could have ruined Harold Souther's career. One day, Harold asked if he could borrow my car. This wasn't an uncommon request. We both used the car frequently, and I was always glad to share it with him. He wanted to take Lucille Killingsworth to Seminole to see her mother. I presumed he knew they would need special permission to go out of town, since Lucille was a freshman.

Seminole was about twenty-five miles south of Shawnee and Harold easily made it in forty-five minutes. They had a delightful visit with Lucille's mother in the afternoon and she prepared a gourmet dinner for them. After dinner they drove around the village so Lucille could show Harold where she went to school and church. As the sun was making its journey to the west, Harold decided it was time to head for Shawnee.

It's difficult to think of anyone getting lost in Seminole, but lost they got. It seemed to be taking a long time to get to the highway and there were no street-lights or signs to help. They thought at any moment they would come to the highway. By now it was pitch dark and the narrow road came to a dead end. Harold asked, "Which way do we turn?" Lucille didn't know and she said, "Harold, I'm lost." Harold said, "That makes two of us!" Harold figured he needed to turn left, which was exactly the wrong decision.

Harold quickly noticed that the fuel gauge was on "empty." Here they were in the middle of nowhere and driving on fumes. They had seen nothing resembling a gas station since they left Seminole, and that was a long time ago. They continued for several miles with no signs of civilization. The engine gauge sounded like it was gasping for fuel, then it stopped. They were out of gas, lost in a dark world, and no signs of houses or farms. They must have felt desperate!

Harold pushed the car to the side of the road. They locked the car, and started walking. It was so dark, they could hardly see their feet or the road. Harold said they must have walked for miles before they saw a farmhouse. Dogs began barking and they became afraid. They slowly approached the door and Harold knocked – surely they would face the business end of a gun or rifle. The door opened and indeed a farmer was there with a shotgun in his hand. He demanded, "Who are you and what do you want?"

They meekly explained they were students from Oklahoma Baptist University and that they had become lost on their way from Seminole, and had run out of gas. Before Harold stopped talking, he got the nerve to ask the man if he had any gasoline. The man replied, "No." Harold then asked if he knew where he might get gasoline, and again the answer, "No." In desperation Harold asked if they had a phone, and the answer a third time, "No, and there isn't a phone anywhere near here." Harold knew only one more question to ask, "Sir, would you let us spend the night, possibly a room for Lucille, and let me sleep on the sofa in your living room, or even on the floor?"

The man talked with his wife and in a moment he came back and said, "You young people are sure in a dilemma. It's against my judgment to do this (their hearts began to sink) but, we believe you, and we are willing to let you stay here tonight. Lucille, you can sleep in the bedroom, which opens to this room. Harold, you can sleep on the sofa over there, and I will sleep on a folding bed that I will place just outside the door to Lucille's room. I will have my shotgun by my side. I am doing this, not because I do not trust you, but I dare say, my testimony may be needed to help you explain all this to Dr. Raley. In the morning we will have an early breakfast, and then take you in our horse-drawn wagon to get some gasoline and to find your way to Shawnee."

Harold and Lucille then learned that this gracious man and his wife had children who were graduates of OBU and were acquainted with Dr. Raley, the president. The farmer also told them he was a deacon in a nearby country Baptist church. Harold said that before they retired they had a prayer meeting with the farmer and his wife. For Harold and Lucille it was a "praise meeting."
They were thankful to be safe, but they knew they were in deep trouble. They had broken two rules, about which the administration was very firm. First, they had left Shawnee without permission; this was a rule of the women's

dormitory. Second, they had passed the curfew time for a dormitory student to be out of the dorm.

Meanwhile, several of us at OBU were concerned and worried about them. We knew that this was out of character for both of them. I was afraid that they had been in an accident, or had been attacked in some way. We even contacted the police in Seminole to see if they knew anything about them. It was a long night waiting for their return and to hear they were all right.

When Harold and Lucille returned to OBU, they went directly to the office of the Dean of Women, Mrs. Earle. She was by no means sympathetic. She immediately began to recite the rules, emphasizing the graveness of their irresponsibility. Mrs. Earle called Dr. Raley's office and reported their return and their likely story. Dr. Raley told her to bring both of them to his office immediately. He had summoned the Discipline Committee, and they were waiting to begin their investigation.

Again Harold and Lucille related their story in detail. The committee reminded them of the critical nature of their situation and that two classmates had been expelled for a similar offense a few weeks ago. The committee asked many questions trying to find a flaw in their story. Then, they told Harold and Lucille, "We need some time to investigate your claims. For the time being, you should not return to classes until further notice."

Harold and Lucille apologized for their misdeeds and appealed for mercy. They tried to assure the committee that there was no sexual impropriety involved in this incident. Harold appealed to them to talk with the farmer and his wife; he gave their names and address to the committee. Lucille told the committee that she didn't stop to think that Seminole was outside of the OBU area. She said, "We had no intention of returning after the curfew. We were the victims of circumstances beyond our control as far as this was concerned."

Two weeks went by and they heard nothing from the committee. Harold and Lucille were devastated. In spite of the fact they couldn't attend classes, they kept up with their studies and projects.

Finally, they were called to appear before the committee. Dr. Raley presided. He explained the careful and prayerful way in which the committee had worked. He congratulated Harold and Lucille for the way they conducted themselves during this precarious situation. He said, "You were fortunate to have fallen in the hands of two most gracious people. Not many would have opened their door to you, not to mention taking you in for the night, feeding you breakfast, taking you for a horse and buggy ride, helping you get gasoline for your car, and then directing you to Shawnee. We thank God for your safe return. We find you as not responsible for not returning to Shawnee that night. However, we cannot overlook the fact that you broke the rules relative to leaving Shawnee without permission. This applies directly to Lucille and indirectly to Harold as accessory. Harold and Lucille, you are both forbidden to visit with one another for the rest of this semester. This means on or off campus. As a judge would say, 'Case closed.' You both need to send 'thank you' notes to the farmer and his wife. They saved your skins and possibly your careers!"

There was much rejoicing in all our hearts, although Harold and Lucille couldn't talk with one another. All of us thanked God for answered prayer. Harold and Lucille said, "There was a lot of praying going on in our hearts on that dark night and particularly when we approached the door of that farmhouse."

We told them we had been praying back in Shawnee since we were in the dark about their safety. And, all of us were praying that the committee would deal fairly with our friends.

The spring and fall of my last year at OBU went by in rapid speed. They were busy days. So much was packed in those five months: Our trips each weekend to South Central Oklahoma, the performance of "Martha" in the early spring, and the Easter Cantata that was broadcast over the Oklahoma Mutual Radio Network.

SOME OBU GIANTS

In listing OBU giants I must mention my voice teacher, Ruth Mitchell Roesch. God used her to change the direction of my life. I owe her so much. She was the lady who first discovered my singing voice. By her teaching, training, encouragement, and patience, she led me to find "God's plans for me, my life, my hope, and my future." Ruth Mitchell Roesch directed all of the major productions.

The organist for the two oratories was Warren Angell. He had been a professor of piano and organ before becoming the Dean of the College of Fine Arts. He also founded the Bison Glee Club of which I was a charter member. The Dean, as he was affectionately called, taught us to sing with a special touch of style and harmony that was unique. Few, if any, were equal to his caliber in that day.

The Dean possessed a spirit of love and joy, splashed with an extra measure of energy and enthusiasm. His life radiated with a trust in God and the empowerment of the Holy Spirit. He was a godly man. Only eternity will reveal the vast impact of this man on the music ministry of Southern Baptist churches and institutions. Many OBU music graduates now preside as ministers of music in churches all over this nation and around the world. Others are teaching music in colleges and seminaries.

His contagious smile and the twinkle of his eyes, revealed to all that he was a man who sincerely loved music. He had respect for the old songs, but God inspired him to write many new songs and anthems. In 1937 he wrote the "OBU Hymn." He also wrote two anthems, which he dedicated to the Sanctuary Choir of Bellevue Baptist Church of Memphis, Tennessee. Years later when he was in his 90s, he was still smiling, playing the piano, writing new music, giving concerts, and encouraging his former students to carry on for the Lord.

Another OBU giant was Dr. James N. Owens – quite possibly one of the most popular men on the faculty, but very few would know him by the above name. He was known simply as, Uncle Jimmy. He taught German and Spanish. I took two years of Spanish from him, but I don't remember much. What stands out in my mind are the hours I spent in the rocking chair in his office listening to his advice. He wasn't an official counselor, but he always had very practical solutions for the problems students faced. He would say, "If you want to be happy, go out and render service for the Lord." His multitude of friends bear witness that he practiced what he preached.

The last, but by no means the least, was a team of two giants: Dr. and Mrs. John W. Raley. Dr. Raley was installed as president of OBU the year I arrived. He came from a pastorate in Bartlesville, Oklahoma, and was thoroughly committed to Christian education. He called it "Education Plus." He wanted the world to know that OBU offered not only the best in education, but also an environment where Christ was honored and the Bible was looked upon as the Divine Word of God. He could be firm when he needed to be, but even then he never lost his composure or his smile.

His wife, Helen, was a charming and gracious first lady of the University. She knew most students by name and her thoughtfulness was admired by all who knew her. When she learned something about a student's family she never forgot it. She also expressed appreciation to people who served or made contributions to the university or her family. Two of my sons attended OBU and whenever I saw Mrs. Raley, she would ask about them by name. Wasn't God good to surround me with these wonderful giants?

Mom and dad on wedding day

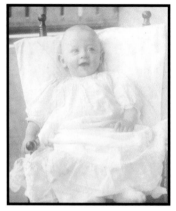

8 months

age 3, right

Mother

Grandma Bailey

1st tricycle, age 4

age 2

age 7

age 12

Firechief, age 9

Boy Scouts Band - I am the trumpet player to the right of the drummer

1st suspenders

*Jim Savage, Harold Souther, Elmer Bailey,
& Chuck Wilson*

Me, Mom, Dad, Harold Souther

*Double dating in the high school days...
Harold Souther, Mary Louise Stout,
Virginia Stapleton, & me*

Elmer and his 2 brothers,
Don & Carroll.

OBU Male Quartet
Collegiate Favorite Of The Southland

Forest Stith - 1st tenor; Jack Dodgen - 2nd tenor;
Elmer Bailey - baritone; Raymond Hall - bass

Bailey family as we arrived at Bellevue Baptist Church in 1960

Elmer, Ramsey, Virginia, Roger, & Jim

Virginia's Parent's - The Shipmans

*my wife's mom,
sister Sue, & father Jim*

*Rev. Wilbur McDaniel
(my 1st pastor)
Avondale Baptist Church -
Chattanooga, TN*

Dr. Warren Angell

My hero, B.B. McKinney

Dr. Homer Lindsay
(my 2nd pastor)
1st Baptist Church -
Jacksonville, FL

Dr. Ramsey Pollard
(my 3rd pastor)
Broadway Baptist Church -
Knoxville, TN
& Bellevue Baptist Church -
Memphis, TN

Executive Staff at Bellevue in 1981

Dr. Jim Whitmire, Dr. Tommy Lane, Dr. Adrian Rogers,
Bob Sorrell, & Elmer Bailey

Staff

Diane Mills, Linda Glance, Velma Rhea Torbet, Eloise Hatfield

*Three Veteran Religious Educators
representing more than 150 years of service*

Henry Love, Windy Rich, & Elmer Bailey

*Recognizing the important role of ministers of education in Southern
Baptist life, LifeWay Church Resources selected Elmer Bailey and
Windy Rich as exemplary examples of that key office and honored both
at the Annual State Leaders Banquet in Nashville, Tennessee in 2000.
Henry Love, another veteran Christian educator is pictured with
Bailey and Rich.*

*William Taylor,
Sunday School Leaders,
Lifeway Christian Resources
of the Southern Baptist Convention*

CHAPTER SIX

SUMMER FOLLOWING GRADUATION FROM OBU

Graduation came and went. I now held an AB Degree from OBU. How proud I was to be known as an alumnus of the school that had made such an impact on my life, Oklahoma Baptist University. After graduation I was asked to spend the summer with the Male Quartet – giving concerts and doing promotion work for the school. First, we first went northwest from Shawnee, then west to the Panhandle. We gave concerts in forty churches in over a ten-week span. We ended our summer tour at the famous Falls Creek Assembly. At that time it was probably the largest church-related retreat center in the world with between eighteen and twenty thousand visitors every year.

Our time at Falls Creek gave me opportunity to meet some outstanding personalities like B. B. McKinney, who was in charge of music for the Southern Baptist Convention. He was also one of Southern Baptists' most prolific song-writers. If you pick up most any Southern Baptist hymnal, you'll discover they contain many of his songs and choruses. Most gospel hymnals also contain one or more of his songs. He introduced two of his best-loved songs during our time at Falls Creek: "Breathe On Me" and "Wherever He Leads, I'll Go."

We were thrilled when Dr. McKinney asked our quartet to introduce a new hymn he had written called "Falls Creek." From that moment on, Dr. McKinney and I became good friends. I took part in many of his conferences on music across the country. If I were present, he would call me to the platform to sing and I usually chose one of his songs. He always told me, "Sing with your heart, as unto the Lord." The music God placed on his heart has been a blessing to Bible-believing people around the world. I thank God that His plans for me included my association with B. B. McKinney, a dear sweet friend. God bless his memory.

Now, back to the summer of 1938. Out of the blue sky, I received a "Dear John" letter from Fern Long. I felt the whole world come down around me. I was sure that I loved her, and she had given me every evidence that she loved me, as well. I tried to call her, but never could reach her. I wrote letters pleading with her to reconsider and I never received an answer. I grieved for weeks; I couldn't think of anything else.

Thank God for my friends in the quartet. They showed their concern and comforted me. Their biggest help was to remind me of the words of one of our quartet numbers, "My Heavenly Father Watches Over Me" by Charles H. Gabriel (© 1938, Homer Rodeheaver):

I trust in God wherever I may be;
Upon the land or on the rolling sea.
For come what may from day to day;
My heavenly Father watches over me.

They also pointed out my life verse, Jeremiah 29:11, which I shared as part of my testimony at every concert. These things all brought me back to my senses. I still was hurting but I knew all was right, and God would take care of me. And did He ever! Never in a lifetime would I have had the opportunity to get the precious jewel God had for me if I had married Fern. God had other plans. He doesn't reveal all of the future to us, but He is always there and working out His plans for our future.

As our summer closed the quartet all went their separate ways. I headed to my new home in Hollywood, Florida and my new mom! Over the summer, my dad married a lovely lady named Claire. She had been a widow for 25 years and Dad a widower for 30 years. After they married, they moved from Michigan to Florida. I was so happy for Dad, and I enjoyed getting to know Claire. She was a delightful woman. Dad had 25 years with my mother and 25 with Claire.

I didn't have but two weeks to visit with Dad and Claire before I had to leave for Southwestern Seminary in Fort Worth, Texas (the largest seminary in the world). The campus is on the highest level of land in Fort Worth. It is known as "the Hill." I had the opportunity to study with men and women who are legends of Southern Baptist history such as Dr. Lee R. Scarborough, Dr. B. A. Copass, Dr. W. T. Connor, Dr. Edwin McNeely, Dr. William Howse, and many others.

The one who meant the most was my voice teacher, Dr. McNeely, affectionately known as Mac. He was more than just a voice teacher, he was a philosopher, humorist, and counselor. He cared tenderly for all his pupils. When I had a problem, he would put his arm around my shoulder and pray earnestly for me. Then, he'd give me suggestions for solutions.

THE CALL TO AVONDALE

Shortly after I went to seminary, I received a call from a Rev. Wilbur McDaniel, Pastor of Avondale Baptist Church of Chattanooga, Tennessee, inviting me to lead the music in a revival in his church. He said, "Dr. Ramsey Pollard is the evangelist." I immediately knew who had recommended me. He continued, "I also want you to pray about the possibility of joining my staff as Minister of Education and Music, the Lord willing, of course." I was so excited I wanted to shout! Could it be the Lord was answering a prayer of my heart? I believe Dr. McNeely was helping me to find what God wanted me to do in His service. I could hear Him calling, "Follow Me."

At this time, Billy Souther was the Minister of Education and Music at Tabernacle Baptist Church in Fort Worth, where Dr. Pollard was pastor. When I was in the Male Quartet, we gave a concert there and I stayed in the Pollard home. I developed blood poisoning in my foot – it was swollen and red streaks were going up my leg. The Pollards took me to an emergency clinic. When I told the doctor I had to leave the next morning for concert engagements, he said, "No Way! Your quartet has just become a trio. You cannot leave until this blood-poisoned foot is cleared up." The other members of the quartet went on without me. I stayed with the Pollards for a little more than a week and rode with them to the Southern Baptist Convention. We got there just in time for me to sing with the quartet at the convention.

Was it not remarkable how God used these friendships to help me on my spiritual journey? Who was involved? God, of course, using Harold Souther, Billy Souther, Dr. and Mrs. Pollard, my professors, Ralph Pardee, Dr. and Mrs. Savage in Pontiac, and also countless friends who were praying for me.

I accepted the call to Avondale, but I believe Wilbur McDaniel didn't have a clue as to what I was to do as the Minister of Education and Music, and neither did I. I knew a little more about music, but practically nothing about education. In the courses I took in seminary and at OBU, it was mostly philosophy and theory. I had a God-given talent in music, but had to learn the hard way about education.

GOD REVEALS THE PRECIOUS JEWEL
HE HAD RESERVED FOR ME

The pianist at Avondale was Stella Craft. She was a fun-loving person who enjoyed getting young people together for fellowship every Sunday evening after church, and every Wednesday evening after choir rehearsal. She invited me to join the gang. I remember the first time I went out with them. It was a small group including Stella, Kenneth and Betty Hill, Sue and Virginia Shipman, Doris Bright and others. I was especially attracted to Virginia Shipman. I invited her to go to a movie the very next week. I didn't have a car, so we had to take the streetcar to downtown Chattanooga. I didn't know it yet, but she was the precious jewel God had reserved for me.

Virginia and I began dating on a steady basis. She was pretty as a picture, full of fun, and sharp as a tack. More than that, she loved the Lord with all her heart, was well acquainted with the Bible, and was filled with good teaching ideas. She actually put me to shame when it came to memorizing Scriptures. I thought to myself, "She would make a good wife for a minister."

At the time, I was living with George and Mary Edgemon. They were so gracious to let me live with them. Mary often asked me to join them for breakfast. One morning after breakfast when George had gone to work, Mary said, "Brother Bailey, I know it is none of my business, but I feel led of the Lord to talk with you about a matter." She continued, "What are your intentions about Virginia?" I was surprised and perplexed at her question. I said to her, "She is a lovely girl, we are good friends, and that's about it." Mrs. Edgemon replied, "I happen to know she is head over heels in love with you. She needs to know where you stand. If you're not interested in her you ought to break it off, but if you're serious about her, you couldn't find a more precious wife than her." I know that God was speaking to me through Mary Edgemon. I could tell by the way she presented this difficult scenario. She awakened me to the fact that Virginia was the precious jewel that God had reserved for me.

That very next night Virginia and I went to a Nelson Eddy movie. On the way home I told her that I loved her, and if she felt the same, I would be pleased if she would marry me. There was no one in the trolley car but the conductor and the two of us. She said, "Elmer, I do love you, and I say yes, yes, yes! I thought you would never ask!" Well, that became one hot trolley!

We decided this would be our little secret until after we talked with her parents. Mr. Shipman was highly respected not only as a layman of the church, but also as a leader in the community. Her mother Floy was a most wonderful wife and mother, and she too, was held in high esteem in church and the community. Virginia and I were anxious to receive their approval and their blessings.

We also wanted time with Rev. and Mrs. McDaniel, our pastor and his wife. We knew they would give us wise counsel about marriage. We had observed their relationship and their love for one another, and the sweet home they provided their daughter and son. We both were determined that these loved ones should be the first to hear of our plans.

First, we met with Mr. and Mrs. Shipman, so we could share the love that we had for each other and assure them that we were fully committed for the rest of our lives. I'll have to admit I was scared they might say no or not now. I didn't know what the next step would be in those cases. I guess I needed their assurance that this was God's plan for my life, and not just my dream. That assurance came when Jim Shipman said, "Well Elmer, we are not surprised, but we are so pleased. We have been praying about this ever since you started dating Virginia. We are so happy for you both and welcome you with open arms to our family." That's when the kissing and hugging started. Virginia's mother was weeping. I thought she was unhappy about it all. I tried to comfort her by saying, "Mrs. Shipman, don't cry, you are not losing a daughter, you are gaining a son, son-in-law that is." She replied, "Oh Elmer, these are tears of joy. You have made me so happy. I know that God has brought you together." They wanted to tell sister Sue the news, but we wanted to keep this little secret until we talked with Rev. McDaniel and his wife. The Shipmans agreed and we proceeded with the next step.

Wilbur and Mina Lou McDaniel had been such a good example as a husband and wife team. They were thrilled with our news and agreed to be co-counselors in preparation for our marriage. Wilbur promised to "tie a good solid knot." The date was set for July 11, 1941.

The next step was to get the rings. We had very little money, so we went the economy route. Through a jeweler friend in the church and two anonymous people in the choir, we were able to get two wedding bands and an engagement ring with a little diamond. We thought they were beautiful. I still don't know the names of the dear benefactors who gave us such a nice wedding gift!

After the engagement ring was on Virginia's finger we went public on the first Sunday in March 1941. It caused quite a stir for our friends and family. I didn't realize there was so much to do in getting married. It was all beyond me – planning showers for the bride-to-be, selecting the wedding party, printing and mailing wedding invitations, renting tuxedos, and a million other details. Mrs. Shipman and Virginia were working hard to produce the wedding gown and dresses for the bridesmaids. Virginia and her friends joined Sue and her friends to mail about six hundred invitations! I guess it wasn't so hard with the assembly line method.

EXCITING PAGES ABOUT OUR COMING WEDDING

"How great and marvelous is our God." I loved Virginia from the moment I saw her. Without a doubt, God led me to my perfect match. I wouldn't have found her otherwise. There were so many circumstances that could have stood in the way of our meeting. I don't believe it was accidental. I know it was God at work in our lives. No other person in the entire world could have survived my impatience, and my pouting when things didn't go as I planned.

Virginia, without even knowing, was teaching me, even while we were courting, to overcome these weaknesses in my life. It's amazing the insight she possessed and the people skills that God gave her. I don't know how she did it, but she did! She was a far better Bible scholar than I was, though she had never been to seminary. She was self-taught, an avid reader and one who absorbed what she read. While she was in high school she resolved to read the Bible through every year. She kept that resolve all her life, until the last few years when she became too weak.

Virginia had always read the King James Version for her Bible reading. One day I suggested she use a different translation each year. She said, "Okay, if you will read with me." With good intention, I agreed. I had never read the Bible through. I tried many times but was never able to do it. Virginia was a speed-reader and retained what she read, while I was a slow reader and had difficulty remembering. We each had to read at our own speed. I was never able to keep up with her. However, the challenge was profitable for us. I came closer to getting through the Bible than before, and through our Bible reading, we had the opportunity to discuss passages along the way. She was always ahead of me, but she patiently discussed the passage I was on that day.

The work at church was going well, but my responsibilities began to conflict with our wedding preparations. In order to keep our jobs, we both had to revise our schedules to get everything done. I asked the Pastor to let us skip VBS this year because of the wedding and previously planned trip to Ridgecrest.

God was blessing the church in a remarkable way. A spirit of joy and excitement seemed to be prevailing in every area of our ministry. Dr. McDaniel was happy to see this renewal of commitment. The Sunday School team of workers was responding to our training sessions for starting weekly workers' meetings. At the same time we were building a prospect file and program and they were well received.

With Easter Sunday behind us, (the choirs thrilled me as they glorified our risen Lord) we were now in a countdown to July 11. I was so pleased when my brother Carroll called from Hollywood, Florida, to say he would come to the wedding and be my best man. And, more news! He was bringing my dad and new mom with him. I was walking on air. I only wished my brother Don could come, but I didn't know where he was. I hadn't been in touch with him since I went away to college and Dad and Carroll didn't know where he was either.

It would be wonderful if we could all be together for the wedding. I thought my aunts might know Don's whereabouts. I called Aunt Laura and the last she heard, he was playing in an orchestra on a boat from Detroit to Bob-Lo-Park. This gave me another lead. I knew the orchestra director, Buddy Fisher, so I called him. He didn't know either, but he was able to fill in some of Don's history. First, Fisher said Don and his first wife were divorced, but he knew nothing about her whereabouts, or their two children. He also told me that

Don was hitting the bottle and needed help. Before we hung up, he said if I found Don to let him know he needed him in the orchestra.

Aunt Laura called back to say she had found Don and gave me his phone number. I reached him and learned he was working at the Dodge plant in Detroit. He said he had a long bout with liquor, but some of his friends put him in touch with Alcohol Anonymous. Through that program he found God, sought His help, and hadn't had a drink in more than six months. I rejoiced with him about that victory and told him I loved him and wished he could come to my wedding. His work wouldn't permit it, but he said that he hoped to see me after the wedding. I told him that Carroll was going to be my best man, and he was bringing Dad and his new wife, Claire, with him. Don had not heard they had married – how sad that these gaps had occurred in our relationship.

Don told me about his new wife, Dorothy, and he knew we would love her when we met. I told him that was all the more reason why he should come to the wedding and bring Dorothy. Don said, "Elmer I wish I could come, I really do. But, right now it is just impossible. I'm the new kid on the block at work. I know they won't give me time off and I can't afford to lose my job. Plus Dorothy is having problems and I can't leave her. She wouldn't be able to come."

I mentioned that I had talked with Buddy Fisher and that he was trying to track him down to play in his orchestra. Don quickly said, "I'm not interested in his offer. I don't want to be around those people. They wouldn't encourage me in my new lifestyle. Most of them are either alcoholics, drug addicts, or both." I was surprised and pleased by his response and said, "You are exactly right. Stick with your convictions!" He thanked me and let me pray with him. I assured him I would continue praying for him and Dorothy (though he didn't say another word about her problem). When I hung up, I couldn't get Dorothy off my mind. We just had to get together somehow, somewhere, and sometime soon. I tried to get with Don, but between his work schedule and my church tasks, it seemed impossible.

Eventually, I found out why Don wouldn't talk initially about Dorothy's condition. He was embarrassed because she was an alcoholic and drug addict. I asked him if she had sought any help or counseling, and he said she tried, but didn't stay with it. I encouraged him to keep trying; she needed what he had found in Alcoholics Anonymous.

Wedding Party 1941

FRONT ROW: *Flower Girl, Lois Jane McDaniel; Ring bearer, Wilbur McDaniel, Jr.*

SECOND ROW: *Doris Bright, Mary Jo Axmacher, Bernard Clonts, Sue Shipman, Mina Lou McDaniel, Caslo Kidwell, Bette Kepner, Mary Belle Carson.*

THIRD ROW: *Stella Craft, Delmont Wilson, Frances Roy, J. T. Shipman, Carroll Bailey, Betty Hill, Wilbur McDaniel, Kenneth Hill.*

113

CHAPTER SEVEN

MY FIRST VISIT TO RIDGECREST

The week after my wedding, I joined my new pastor, Rev. Wilbur McDaniel for my first trip to the Southern Baptist Conference Center at Ridgecrest. Rev. McDaniel had suggested earlier that he and I should go to Ridgecrest after our revival and the wedding to get up-to-date information about Sunday School work. I had heard of Ridgecrest many times while I was at OBU and Southwestern Seminary and looked forward to the time when I would be able to attend these conferences. This was a thrilling and significant experience for me. The drive was beautiful from Chattanooga through the foothills of the Blue Ridge Mountains. We were both anxious to learn how to build a Sunday School.

Dr. J. N. Barnette led the session on Sunday School growth. He was head of Sunday School work for Southern Baptists. Much of his material came from a book entitled "Building A Standard Sunday School" by Arthur Flake. Dr. Flake was Dr. Barnette's hero and predecessor with the Sunday School board.

During this conference at Ridgecrest I heard of Flake's Formula for the first time in my life: 1) discover the possibilities, 2) enlarge the organization, 3) provide needed space, 4) enlist and train workers, and 5) go after people. Along with these tenets, Dr. Barnett presented the laws of Sunday School growth. These principles were put in place to ensure we did the right things and avoided the wrong things as we followed Flake's Formula.

Briefly, let me say that this formula was the key to the tremendous growth in SBC Sunday School from 1920 to 1950. It was so successful for Southern Baptists that other denominations adopted these principles to build their Sunday Schools. Since then, many of the suggestions by Arthur Flake and J. M. Barnette have been changed and adapted to fit the day and time in which we live. I believe the basics of Sunday School growth in "Building a Standard Sunday School" or "The Pull of the People" (Convention Press revised edition, 1956) are still applicable today.

Dr. Barnette closed the week's study by emphasizing the reasons for visitation and outreach. He emphasized that the Bible commands us to reach out to others. Furthermore, he showed us that Jesus and the New Testament church are our examples and that the lost condition of the multitudes is our incentive.

What a wonderful week! Our notebooks were crammed with notes and our hearts were enthused with the possibilities. Watch out, Avondale Baptist Church. Things were about to happen!

Upon returning home from Ridgecrest, I was so excited about what could be done if we would attempt to follow the Laws of Sunday School Growth and Flake's Formula. I was amazed at the response of the Avondale people. They hadn't been to Ridgecrest, and they hadn't heard the wonderful messages we had heard, but they were determined to do all they could do under the leadership of the Spirit of God to build a Sunday School.

AVONDALE ACCEPTS THE CHALLENGE

Rev. McDaniel and I thought long and hard about all we had learned and just how we would present it. Every Wednesday night, we had a supper in our fellowship hall, so we decided to ask all of our Sunday School department directors to meet on the stage with the curtains closed and eat their meal. Once we prepared the Sunday School superintendent and/or educational directors with their marching orders, they discussed them each Wednesday night. After supper, all the Sunday School workers then went to their Sunday morning room with the department director for department meetings.

The first item on the agenda was a bird's eye view of next Sunday's lesson. There were also opportunities for teachers to discuss any problems they might have with the lesson. Also, the outreach directors of the classes were given opportunities to check on the number of contacts made in the past week and the number of prospects discovered. If they found any prospects, they were assigned to the proper class for visitation the next week.

The War Years

Things rolled along very well for two years until that heartbreaking Sunday afternoon on December 7, 1941, when someone rushed into the choir room to tell us that the Japanese had bombed Pearl Harbor. Hundreds of our troops had been killed. It was the beginning of America's entrance into World War II. In the ensuing days almost all of our young men and middle-aged men were drafted or volunteered for the military service. After only a few months, I was drafted into the US Army. I will never forget that lonely day when we gathered at the Hamilton County Courthouse in Chattanooga to await the trucks that would take us to Fort Oglethorpe.

Induction into the Army involved more than just signing a few papers. It included the official action of induction, a very thorough physical examination, orientation instructions, and issuance of GI equipment including a weapon, clothing, shoes, canteen, tin cup, and other implements for eating, plus a back pack and blanket. Then, to top it all off, a cap. A Sergeant instructed us how to load the pack. He told us to watch carefully because we would be required to place all of our equipment into our pack in a short time.

After the backpacking experience, we were instructed to go to the dining hall for our lunch. While we were in the dining hall, a First Lieutenant came to speak to us. He told us to listen very carefully: "After lunch, you will be given an opportunity to go back to Chattanooga. You can use the phone to call someone in your family to meet you at the Courthouse at a given time." Again, he cautioned us about listening carefully and keeping our mouths shut. He said, "It will be very painful to you if you relay to any of your family or friends any of the information you receive here, even though it may seem very incidental to you. Tell no one where you are or where you are going or when you are going from Fort Oglethorpe. This isn't a request. It is a command. Be certain that you will be severely punished if you do not follow these instructions. Tomorrow morning you will be here by 9:00. That isn't 9:15 or 9:30 or 10:00. It is 9:00 Eastern Standard Time. The trucks will load at the Courthouse and bring you back here and further instructions will be given at that time. This isn't a game. Do not fail to follow these instructions."

What a surprise! None of us expected to be able to go back home before being sent somewhere else. It was a sweet time with our families and at the same time a very sad time. Most of the men lined up at the Courthouse long before the trucks arrived.

When we returned from our reunion, we went through some exercises and drills during the afternoon. Later that day, we were called to assemble at the parade grounds and told to pack all of our belongings in our backpacks because we were leaving that evening to an unannounced destination. Every depot we passed through the night had the name of the town or city covered so that we couldn't tell where we were, but most of us figured out we were going west from Chattanooga. They changed routes several times during the night until we finally reached our destination. Again, they told us that we could not tell anyone we were at Fort Bliss in El Paso – the home of the elite First Cavalry Division, with General Swift as the commanding officer. This aroused a lot of interest from all of us. We thought the Calvary was a thing of the past, but we were wrong!

There was a roll call on the parade ground the morning of the second day. Our commanding officer informed us that we were in the Headquarters Unit of the 3rd Squadron Provisional. He explained that we were a proposed reconnaissance squadron, and our mission was to make a preliminary survey of the territory and resources of the enemy. He further explained, "Our agenda for the next few weeks will be very light. It will include daily exercise sessions, instructions and training – both in the strategy of reconnaissance and discipline. Any time you have other than items on the instruction sheet, can be your own time. You can do what you want, but you have to remain on the base and in your quarters because your instructions could change at any moment."

We then returned to the barracks and chatted with one another about where we were and what we had to do. There came a voice over the front paging system, "Private Elmer Bailey, report to the company clerk." Standing there was a man in a chaplain's uniform who looked very familiar. I fumbled around trying to remember what I was supposed to do when I came face-to-face with an officer. It was Bob Bizzel of Oklahoma – now Major Bizzel. (He had been head of Sunday School work for Oklahoma Southern Baptists prior to volunteering for service in the war. I even sang in this church with the Male

Quartet.) Major Bizzel returned my salute and immediately began talking about how glad he was to see me. If he was glad to see me, I was doubly glad to see him! He asked if I would like to work with him if he could get permission. He said, "Don't get your hopes too high because it is possible that they won't allow it." What a treat to see someone I knew that far away from home!

I was praying with all my might that somehow God would work this out for me. Within two days Major Bizzel found me and said he had permission for me to be an assistant chaplain. At this point I wouldn't receive a change in rank, but I would have many perks that other privates didn't have. I would be exempt from KP, guard duty, maintenance duty, but not from actual training or instruction exercises. I would also have the privilege and honor of eating with the chaplains for all meals. Major Bizzel also put me in charge of music for the chapel services, which he led. This was one of God's beautiful plans for me, and He gave me the choice to follow-through. How could I have done otherwise?

This relatively easy assignment, however, was short-lived because Major Bizzel was transferred out of the reconnaissance group. I was then promoted to Corporal and given the difficult assignment of being in charge of our motor supplies. I knew practically nothing about motor supplies, which included supplies for vehicles and tools for working on the vehicles. My fellow soldiers gave me a great deal of ribbing whenever they came for supplies – they knew I wasn't very well informed. They would come in and ask for a left-handed screwdriver or some other concocted tool that didn't exist, and then they'd leave laughing at my ignorance. But it was all in fun. For the most part, the soldiers I worked with were fairly good guys. Of course, there was one mean-spirited person who I had to ignore.

In order to break the monotony, the Army offered several sports including football, basketball, and volleyball. Polo was even offered for squadrons, like ours that had horses. This was probably the most popular spectator sport on the base.

One day the director of football asked me if I ever did any writing. I told him I did a little editing and writing when I worked in churches. He asked me if I had any experience in sports writing. I told him I hadn't, but that I enjoyed sports, and football was probably my favorite. He said, "Do you think you could write articles about the football games that we have every Sunday afternoon?

These stories would appear in the weekly division paper." After I considered it a while, I told him, "If you get a man from each participating squadron to help me identify the players, then I'll write the newspaper stories, or at least I'll give it a try. If it works, you can keep me. If it doesn't, you can get someone else." I had this fascinating job for the rest of the football season. It gave me opportunity to get acquainted with a lot of the men from other squadrons.

After the football season ended I woke up one morning with a high fever. I thought I had the flu or something similar, but when I got to the hospital, they diagnosed me with spinal meningitis. I slipped into a coma and don't remember anything that happened next. Later, I learned that the doctors quarantined the post, and no one could come in or go out for several weeks. I also learned the tragic news that two other men who had spinal meningitis died shortly after being diagnosed.

General Swift, who was commanding officer of the First Cavalry Division, called my wife in Chattanooga and told her I was in the hospital with spinal meningitis. He said, "Mrs. Bailey, I don't recommend that you come way out here to El Paso. Your husband is in a coma. He will not know you, and you will not be able to communicate with him. In fact, you really can't come onto the post because it is quarantined. I assure you that he is getting the best care that could be found anywhere. I promise I will call you every morning and give you a report on your husband's condition. As soon as the quarantine is lifted I will send you transportation to get to El Paso so you can be with your husband."

The doctors treated me with an experimental drug that had been very successful in treating spinal meningitis. There was no other choice. I regret I had spinal meningitis, but I am glad that my treatment resulted in many going through this disease without incident.

General Swift kept his word and called my wife and as soon as the quarantine was lifted. As he promised, he sent Virginia a round-trip airline ticket from Chattanooga to El Paso. She enjoyed El Paso so much that she decided to stay there until I was discharged.

I was still in the hospital at Christmastime and Christmas morning, I got a surprise visit from a dear friend of mine, Bailey Forrester. I hadn't seen him since we graduated from OBU in 1939. He had become a chaplain in one of the First Cavalry Division groups. We had a wonderful visit, and he had brought some nice gifts for Virginia and me.

I went on furlough to Chattanooga and while I was gone the First Cavalry Division went overseas. I believe they were shipped to the Admiralty Islands in the Pacific. They were involved in many engagements in that area. When the Marines were ready to enter Japan, the First Cavalry Division Reconnaissance Squadrons led the way. They surveyed the land, and reviewed the troops and equipment in Japan. When they were satisfied, they gave the signal for the Marines to advance. This was the beginning of peace.

I was discharged from the Army about two years after the end of the war. At the time, I was stationed in Desert Center, California. As soon as I got my papers, I was on the first train headed to El Paso where Virginia was waiting for me. The train was loaded with troops; there was hardly a place to sit anywhere.

FIRST MINISTRY JOB AFTER THE ARMY

It was time to begin thinking about a job. Avondale Church had found another education and music director, so I put out some feelers to churches that might be interested in a music and education director. I have to admit I made a big error in this search. I was concerned, but I didn't pray about it. I had let myself drift during my years in the Army, and I wasn't praying like I ought. I chose the first church that offered me a job; it was in Port Arthur, Texas. The Lord taught me a lesson in that experience.

As far as church was concerned, I became very unhappy. Personally though, Virginia and I were ecstatic. Our first little baby arrived after we had been in Port Arthur about a year. We named him James Carroll, but we called him Jimmy. Little Jimmy was a precious gift to us from God. He was such a joy. Everyone in the church loved him, and Virginia and I were so proud. Virginia's sister Sue even came to Port Arthur to help us take care of him. His birth helped us realize that we were drifting from the Lord, and so we both recommitted our lives and got back into the center of God's will. God had good plans for us, even though we had made the wrong choices.

REVIVAL IN JACKSONVILLE, FLORIDA

Not long after, I received a call from Dr. Homer Lindsay who was pastor of the First Baptist Church in Jacksonville, Florida. He asked me to lead the music in a revival at his church, and said that Hyman Appleman was to be the evangelist. At the time, Rev. Appleman was probably the most popular of Southern Baptist evangelists. I asked Dr. Lindsay how he happened to call me. He replied, "My good friend Ramsey Pollard recommended you." I told Dr. Lindsay that Dr. Pollard had made a big impact on my life and had recommended me to my first church in Chattanooga. Dr. Lindsay said, "I knew you were at Avondale Church because I was pastor there before Wilbur McDaniel. Your wife Virginia was a little girl when I was there." You see, this was all in God's plans the whole time. It was a plan for my good (as are all of His plans).

Well, I accepted Homer Lindsay's invitation to lead the music, not knowing what God had in store. The revival was one of the most moving experiences in my life since I had been saved. At the end of one week of the revival, Dr. Lindsay said, "We need to go another week." He asked me if I thought I could be away from Port Arthur another week. I called Port Arthur and asked the pastor for permission and he approved.

During this next week, Rev. Appleman approached me and said, "Elmer, my singer who usually works with me has told me he can no longer be on my staff. I have a revival coming up in Kansas City, Missouri, the week after the revival here. I would like to know if you would serve as the singer for that revival. If you can, I will do something I have never done before. I will share the love offering with you on a fifty-fifty basis." He told me that this revival was going to be a citywide revival in a coliseum. Large crowds would be expected and the love offering should be very generous. This, of course, was very attractive to me, but I couldn't feel the Lord was in it.

People were still coming to trust in Christ during this second week, so Dr. Lindsay asked me, "Do you think you can get away for another week?" My pastor balked on this request saying, " You need to get back here. You have been away two weeks." I shared with Dr. Lindsay what my pastor said and what Rev. Appleman had said. I asked Dr. Lindsay for his advice and he said, "You probably would be better off not to go with Hyman Appleman. I have good reasons for making this suggestion, but I don't want to share them with you. Just trust me."

The next day Dr. Lindsay asked me if I would consider becoming his church's education and music director. He said, "I want you to pray about it, and let me know before you leave. If the Lord isn't leading you to do this, then, I wouldn't want you. But if He is in it, I would be proud to have you as my associate." I felt the Lord's peace about leaving Port Arthur. After all, I felt they had been very unfair in not letting me stay on for another week in that great revival. Maybe the Lord was trying to say something to me about this. I called Virginia in Port Arthur and asked her to pray with me. I also told her about Rev. Appleman's invitation and that Dr. Lindsay had asked me to give him a decision before I left the revival.

The next day Virginia called and told me that she had a feeling God was leading us to Jacksonville. She reminded me that Dr. Pollard was the one who had led us to Avondale in Chattanooga and that we had a connection with Dr. Lindsay because he had once been her pastor. I was having a similar prompting from the Holy Spirit, and so I went to Dr. Lindsay and told him we were in accord that God was calling us to Jacksonville and accepted his offer. Next, I called my pastor in Port Arthur and told him that I was giving him two weeks notice effective as soon as I returned to Port Arthur. I would remain on the staff for two weeks, and then I would be coming back to Jacksonville as Dr. Lindsay's associate for education and music. The pastor seemed to be relieved at this news.

THE CALL TO FIRST BAPTIST CHURCH IN JACKSONVILLE

Dr. Lindsay now had an open door to talk to me about financial matters, housing, my job description, and his expectations. I told Dr. Lindsay that I had two big problems for which I needed his help. I didn't own an automobile and we needed a place to live in Jacksonville. Dr. Lindsay said he could help to arrange for me to buy a car. Used cars were very scarce at the time, but he knew some car dealers in his church that he thought would help.

"In the second place," Dr. Lindsay said, "there is a house right next door to me for sale. It isn't an expensive home, and I believe you probably could buy that house if the church helped you with the down payment." I told Dr. Lindsay how much I appreciated his help, but as a war veteran I would probably get some help for a down payment. These were some of the details that Dr. Lindsay and I discussed while I was still in Jacksonville. In the remaining two days I would get Virginia to come by bus to look at the house, and then we would drive back in our own car. We felt the move to Jacksonville was a gift from God. It was in His plan and we made the choice to follow it.

First Baptist Jacksonville had led the Southern Baptist Convention in baptisms for several years, and was known as a growing church. One of Dr. Lindsay's expectations was that I would help the church, and particularly the Sunday School, become aggressively evangelistic. He knew I would need time to plan the music and educational programs. "However," he said, "I want you to spend as much time visiting as you can. I will not be asking you to do anything I am not already doing, and will continue to do. And you can expect me to support you in everything you do as long as you keep me informed as to what you are doing." This excited me even more about our future in Jacksonville.

Virginia came to Jacksonville, just as we agreed, on the Thursday before the end of the revival. We spent the day looking at the house next door to the Lindsays and looking for a car. God had already taken care of a lot of our arrangements, using Dr. Lindsay as a tool. We got the house without any down payment because of the GI Bill. The mortgage was one that would be tight for us, but it was within our budget. A car dealer gave a brand new 1941 Plymouth to the church, which was then assigned to me for my use without any restrictions. We talked with the movers and the church agreed to pay this expense, as well. On Saturday we drove back to Port Arthur in our 1941 Plymouth. Two youngsters and a baby, and we were tickled to death! At every turn God was supplying our needs. This was a definite confirmation of God's will in making this move.

CLOSING REFLECTIONS ABOUT SUNDAY SCHOOL TRAINING

Over the last few years working in various churches, I discovered that Sunday School wasn't the only religious education offered. There was also Baptist Training Union (BYU) or as it was later called, Discipleship Training. For the most part BYPU, BTU, CPU, and other great organizations such as these were going out of style. It was a real tragedy that these effective organizations lost their impact. Many adults in my generation found their places of service in the church – either on staff or in lay leadership through the training received in these organizations. We tried many ways to revitalize that group and bring it back to life, but it was too late.

We lost the organization that maintained a program officially called "Church Training," so other programs began in the churches to train laypersons. Many churches, using the name "Church Training," gave seminars on various subjects, but they didn't provide the member participation we wanted. I believe that is because of the music programs for children and youth that occupied more of their time. I don't mean that as a condemnation, but rather an observation. I praise God for how music programs train children and youth. My church, Bellevue Baptist, has seen the great contribution, which the music program has brought and if you study the curriculum carefully, many good things from "Church Training" have been incorporated. I commend our Minister of Music Jim Whitmire and his staff for seeing that this time is used properly. Our children and youth are involved in the worship services and missions, and they are kept informed of other programs in the church.

CHAPTER EIGHT

THE MIRACLES GOD PERFORMED FOR
FIRST BAPTIST JACKSONVILLE

No doubt about it – First Baptist Church Jacksonville was a miracle church. In His perfect way, God worked to make this church one of the leading churches of the Southern Baptist Convention. In 1939, Dr. Homer Lindsay was called to pastor that church and he accepted knowing that the church was hopelessly in debt due in part to the Great Depression. First Baptist Jacksonville was actually in bankruptcy and many of the decisions regarding the future of the church were made in Bankruptcy Court. As I understand it, the Gulf Life Insurance Company bought the church and its eight-story educational building, then gave back the auditorium and its basement, as well as some room that was back of the church for educational space. Gulf Life then used the education building as a part of their operations.

Dr. Lindsay led First Baptist Jacksonville to make great sacrifices in order to do what God wanted them to do. He was a well-versed man in religious education and was sold on the fact that by building a great Sunday School you can build a great church. He knew that new classes and departments needed to be added as soon as possible.

There was hardly any space, but we kept on growing and added curtains to partition the auditorium for a dozen or more Sunday School classes. We had Sunday School classes in the choir loft and in locations all over downtown Jacksonville. A large men's class met in a building across the street from the auditorium and several classes were in funeral homes nearby. We even rented a building, which I think the church finally bought, that we used for the young people's Sunday School. Our college and career groups met in the YWCA building, which was several blocks from the church. I think the children's ministry suffered the most during this transition. The preschool area was much too small and was located just back of the choir loft in the basement.

Years later, Gulf Life vacated the eight-story building and built a larger building in the adjacent area. Then, this building became too small for them and they built a skyscraper across the river in South Jacksonville. I don't know how it happened, but First Baptist was able to get all of the property that Gulf Life had been using. With this added space the church really began to grow.

This is one of the most intriguing stories of church growth I have ever heard. God worked things out so that a church could do what He wanted them to do. It was certainly a miracle. The work of Dr. Lindsay carried on – first, with the calling of his son, Homer, Jr. as co-pastor. Then, after Dr. Lindsay's death, the church called Dr. Jerry Vines as the new pastor. Today, First Baptist Jacksonville owns much of the land in the downtown area and has an auditorium, which seats 10,000 people (it is filled every Sunday). I thank God for the history of this great church. God was in every move and the victories along the way were won for His glory as thousands came to Jesus Christ.

DR. HOMER LINDSAY PROVIDES HUMBLE LEADERSHIP

In the years before I came to First Baptist Jacksonville, the church had formed a Board that controlled the church. These men were not in attendance at church, but were very active in running the activities of the church. For more than five years, Dr. Lindsay tried to change the policies to get rid of this administrative travesty. All the while, he worked with a humble spirit, a sweet smile, and a devotion to God. He knew that some way and some day the Lord would intervene.

Sure enough, on the fourth attempt to change these policies, the church voted to dispense with the Board and to elect Deacons for three-year terms. After their terms were over, they would rotate off and couldn't come back on the deacon body until after a full year. At this point, Dr. Lindsay became the Pastor of First Baptist Church Jacksonville, Florida. It was the beginning of "God-blessed" period of growth and progress. God surely had plans for this church.

Homer Lindsay was an unusual man. He was a great preacher of the Gospel, a fantastic administrator, and was in great demand as an evangelist around the country. What a privilege I had to serve with him for four years. He was so knowledgeable about the field of education and he taught me many things about building a Sunday School. I believe the key to all the things that happened at First Baptist Jacksonville was a praying pastor working together with a praying people to enlarge the Sunday School organization, find prospects, and provide multiple Bible study opportunities with new classes and departments starting almost weekly.

Dr. Lindsay also believed in visitation and was personally very active in it. He insisted that his staff members also be very involved in this person-to-person activity. I don't think he was a "slave driver." Rather, I believe he was a torchbearer.

MY MINISTRY AT FIRST BAPTIST JACKSONVILLE

I spent a great portion of my time directing the music – this was my one big choir. Let me tell you about a funny incident that happened one Wednesday night at choir rehearsal. I was rearranging the seating of the choir and I placed a lady who had been on the third row of the choir to the back row. She moved a few steps and then she picked up a hymnal and threw it at me. It didn't hit me, but it hit the organist and brought a big cheer from the choir. The lady left the choir loft in a huff and did not return until I left.

Our family expanded again while we were in Jacksonville. Our second son arrived we named him Roger Bradley. What a joyous day that was for Virginia and me! Now, Jimmy had a little brother.

AN UNEXPECTED CALL

In 1947, the building committee was meeting to study plans for a new pre-school building. They had invited me to take part in the planning session, since I had done a lot of preliminary work. We were meeting in a conference room just off the church offices and I heard the telephone ring and the secretary answered. In a few moments she came to the room and said, "Mr. Bailey, there is a Rev. Pollard from Knoxville on the line who wants to talk to you. Do you want to talk to him now, or should I ask him to call back?" I told her I would talk with him, so I excused myself from the committee for a few minutes.

When I answered, it was Dr. Ramsey Pollard. He said, "Elmer, I need your help desperately." I replied, "What can I do for you, Dr. Pollard?" He said, "My educational director just resigned and I need you to come and help me." I said, "Dr. Pollard, I have been with Homer Lindsay for several years now. You recommended me here and we are right in the middle of a building program. I feel it would be unfair for me to leave them right at this time." Dr. Pollard came back and said, "Elmer, I am serious about this matter. I do need you now. Please see if you can find it in the will of God to leave Jacksonville and come to Knoxville."

I told him Virginia and I would need to do a lot of praying about the matter and that I wouldn't consider changing churches unless I had the clear leadership of the Lord. Dr. Pollard understood and said, "God has put it upon my heart to call you, and I hope you find it in His will to come." I asked for time to talk with Virginia and assured him I would get back to him as soon as I had some kind of answer for him.

I was stunned. I had to sit down and wait awhile before I went back to the committee meeting. When I returned, Dr. Lindsay had dropped in for a little while. I told him, "I just talked to Dr. Pollard and he asked me to give his regards to you." Dr. Lindsay was glad to hear from Dr. Pollard and asked me what was on his mind. I said, "You won't like it, but Dr. Pollard asked me to come to Knoxville as his minister of music and education." Dr. Lindsay said, "Well, that old so-and-so, trying to get you away from me." I assured him that Dr. Pollard wasn't trying to get me away from him, but rather he asked me to pray about whether or not God wanted me to serve on his staff (there is a difference you know). I said, "I would never think about going to another church unless God was leading me to make that decision. Dr. Pollard asked me to pray about it, and I certainly will pray and I'll ask Virginia to join me. I have no idea what decision I'll make. I don't want to leave Jacksonville, and I'll have to be convinced that God wants me to leave."

After the meeting, and I called Virginia and told her about Dr. Pollard's call. She said, "I don't want to leave Jacksonville; I like it here and I believe this is where God wants us." I replied, "Virginia, I like it here too, and I don't want to leave, but I think in respect to Dr. Pollard we must pray about this matter and find God's will."

God started working on Virginia, and me as well, about the matter. More and more we felt that God was calling us to Knoxville. I told Virginia that the issue wasn't that we didn't want to go to Knoxville, rather the issue was whether God wanted us to go. In a few days Virginia and I both came to the decision that we needed to go and help Dr. Pollard. A few days later I resigned at Jacksonville, giving them two-weeks notice, and called Dr. Pollard and told him of our decision.

Dr. Pollard was thrilled and he assured me that he would give me his full support in my work. He said, "I know what you have done at Jacksonville and Avondale. You know what to do, and I believe in you. All I will ask is that you keep me informed as to what you are planning and where you are going in assisting our people."

Dr. Pollard said he would make arrangements for our move to Knoxville and would let us know what moving company would be handling the move. I told him I was driving a car that belonged to First Baptist Jacksonville and that I would need to buy a car. He said, "Son, don't worry about that. We'll see that you get a car that you can handle with monthly payments." He also made arrangements for us to rent a house so we wouldn't have to look for a place when we arrived.

When the people at First Baptist Jacksonville heard the news that we were leaving they expressed their regrets with calls and letters. The church gave us a very lovely "going away" party followed by a send-off on a Sunday morning. Dr. Lindsay said many very gracious things about the work we had done and how much he loved us. He assured us that he and the church would be praying for our family. And we headed to Knoxville.

CHAPTER NINE

BROADWAY YEARS

The Pollards and Broadway Baptist Church gave us a royal welcome when we arrived in Knoxville. The first night, a group from the choir greeted us with a serenade. It was so surprising and glorious that the whole neighborhood turned out to see what was going on.

I spent my early days at Broadway looking at ways to grow our Sunday School. One of the laws of Sunday School growth is to continually start new units. Dr. Barnette said, "New units grow faster, win more people to Christ and provide more workers." I started my growth plan by studying the Sunday School and Church Training attendance and enrollment figures (they are a very good indication as to the health of a church). As I compared these figures with the demographic statistics of the area in which Broadway Baptist was located, I discovered that we were hardly reaching these people. One idea I had to reach out to the community was to organize a young married department. I knew that Virginia was very interested in young married couples from our experience in Jacksonville and I asked her to direct this new area of ministry.

In addition, I decided to build a college ministry since we were right in the middle of the University of Tennessee campus. We were reaching only a few UT students at the time, and looking at figures from other churches in the area, I discovered that there were very few who had a significant number of UT students enrolled. This seemed to be a "field that was ripe for harvest." I asked Mrs. Pollard to be the director and found workers for both of these new departments. Not only did I train the new workers on a series of Wednesday nights, but I also encouraged all the Sunday School workers to attend our weekly workers meeting.

While all this was going on, I made plans for a Sunday School Advancement Week. During this week we brought in a group of experienced Sunday School workers for each age division to train our workers. I told the specialists our need to exhort our workers about the importance of reaching out to prospective members who were inactive church members or unchurched in the community.

On the closing Sunday of this Advancement Week program we took a survey of our community to discover people who were not enrolled in Sunday School or attending church anywhere. Next, I went through our membership roll to discover people who were members of the church, but not enrolled in Sunday School. These names, along with the survey names, were compiled into a prospect list. Next, we classified each name by age, and then assigned them to a Sunday School class and department. Dr. Pollard supported these moves with whole-hearted participation and encouragement.

On January 2, 1949, our third son Richard Ramsey Bailey was born. Our joy was complete, as was our family circle. By now, Jimmy and Roger were four and two years of age, respectively.

Broadway Church was already serving a Wednesday night supper in order to increase the attendance at the Wednesday evening service. We changed the format of that supper to some degree in order to use the supper to enhance our weekly workers meeting. Dr. Pollard agreed to excuse the Sunday School workers from the Wednesday night service so that each department could meet during that time. I had done the same sort of meeting in Jacksonville, and it worked well. As before, the workers would eat together, then have their weekly workers meeting. We found people coming to that workers meeting and dinner in larger numbers than before. After about two months, I decided to meet with only the department directors over dinner, and then they would convene with their workers afterward.

This proved to be a very efficient way to carry on the business of the Sunday School departments. Each week, the departments addressed improvements in teaching, outreach development, and promotion of the Sunday School program. They also made a real effort to observe the annual promotion from one department to the other according to age-range assignments.

Not long after we started this weekly workers meeting, our Sunday School classes started to grow. The classes were organized and excited about outreach. Often, Dr. Pollard would mention the importance of the weekly workers meeting on Sundays. Each week our church paper would carry information about the Sunday School work.

Using these strategies we grew from a Sunday School of approximately 800 to over 1,000 in attendance. The workers began seeing the results of their work, and the excitement continued as we grew even more. These changes in our strategy and way of doing things didn't just happen. Every facet of this program entailed a tremendous amount of work by our secretarial staff, department directors, and the workers.

It wasn't long before we needed additional space. To that end, the church built an addition to the existing sanctuary. Our young married class kept growing as well, so we acquired and refurbished a grocery store building that was contiguous to the church property. In another year Broadway Baptist had grown to over 3,000 in Sunday School attendance each week.

One big factor in the growth of Broadway was the fellowship. Our biggest social event each year was the Harvest Festival (Virginia and Mrs. Pollard were the driving forces.) It was a banquet sponsored by the young married division, but included all of the church. As a part of the festival we celebrated wedding anniversaries, engagements, and births. One facet of the program was the dedication of the new babies.

The Sunday School Board in Nashville started observing what was happening with our Sunday School growth, especially the young married department. At the time the Sunday School Board didn't promote or train leadership for young married people. They sent a group of their workers to Broadway to observe what was going on, then asked Virginia to come to Ridgecrest and explain our program at a Sunday School Conference.

For the next twelve years, we kept on growing. My, how God blessed Broadway Baptist Church! I think it was a highlight in our work. Broadway was one church that stayed with the basics of Sunday School work and observed the "laws" of Sunday School growth. The Sunday School Board frequently called upon our staff members to conduct conferences at Ridgecrest and Glorieta Assemblies.

In 1960, our family and the Pollard family went to the lovely Greystone Hotel in Gatlinburg for a fun and restful week – it was just what we needed. One day, we were eating lunch when the waiter told Dr. Pollard that he had a telephone call. He excused himself from the table to take the call. Upon his return he was unusually quiet. At the end of the meal, he shared with us the nature of the call asked all of us to keep in complete confidence the information he was about to share. He said the phone call was from Dr. R. G. Lee, pastor of Bellevue Baptist Church in Memphis and that Dr. Lee asked to meet him the next day at the Knoxville airport conference room.

Dr. Lee told him, "I am asking you as sincerely as I can not to talk to anyone about this, none of your friends or any of your loved ones. Just keep it to yourself until it becomes public news." Dr. Lee then revealed that he planned to retire in a few weeks. "Our Pulpit Committee is working hard, and they are ready to ask you to be the next pastor of Bellevue Baptist Church. They certainly have my hearty and positive response to their intentions," said Dr. Lee. Dr. Pollard was shocked. He thought Dr. Lee would probably be pastor of Bellevue for many more years. He was strong and healthy. He said he felt that God was leading him to make the decision he had made, however, and that the Pulpit Committee had been in prayer and felt, without exception, that they were led to call Dr. Pollard.

Before lunch was over, Dr. Pollard said, "Della and I will fly to Knoxville in the morning to meet Dr. Lee, and Elmer, you have your car and you can get your family home, and Imogene (the Pollards' daughter) can take our group back to Knoxville. Please, I beg of you, do not say a word to anyone about this matter. Nothing has been settled yet and I have not accepted this call. I had been prepared to stay on at Broadway for the rest of my ministry, but we are going to leave this matter in the hands of the Lord. We don't want the community or the church to hear that I may be leaving Broadway and going to Bellevue in Memphis. Just tell people you do not know if they ask. That certainly is true because I do not know!"

This news certainly put a damper on our little party. We were all in a state of shock and found ourselves praying that God wouldn't let it happen. Everyone across the state seemed to be calling Dr. Pollard to ask him whether he was going to Memphis. Dr. Pollard continued to play it cool and responded that he didn't know: "Yes, Bellevue has called me; no, I have not in any way told them yes or no. I am happy in Knoxville and would like to stay here the rest of my life, but we must leave that decision to the Lord. That's what I am trying to do, and I hope you will support me with your prayers."

There were many differences between Dr. Lee and Dr. Pollard. Dr. Pollard said, "I am sure that some of these differences will be so great as to bring about division in the congregation. I would never want to harm the fellowship of the church. The only way I would take this new church call is to have definite call from the Lord in such a way that I know it is God calling me and not just the people."

When Dr. Pollard resigned to go to Bellevue Baptist Church in 1960, Broadway called me as interim pastor, and I served in that capacity for a few months before I joined Dr. Pollard at Bellevue.

CHAPTER TEN

BELLEVUE YEARS

Our first day in Memphis was also Dr. Pollard's first day as pastor. There was a streamer in the sanctuary that said it was Ramsey Pollard Day, officially proclaimed by Memphis and Knoxville mayors. *The Bellevue Messenger* carried a full column tribute to him from the Knoxville Mayor, John Duncan, who opened with this statement:

WHEREAS, Dr. Ramsey Pollard has served Broadway Baptist Church for more than twenty years, and during this time he has been recognized for his leadership by serving in many high offices of the Baptist denomination, and is now serving as President of the Southern Baptist Convention.

He closed his column by saying:

Now therefore, I John J. Duncan, Mayor of the City of Knoxville, do hereby proclaim Friday, February 26, 1960, Dr. Ramsey Pollard Day for his untiring devotion to the great call which he has served, for the task he has taken with enthusiasm and brought to the end of his long career with Broadway Baptist Church, leaving us with the legacy of a large knowledge of our greatest book, the Bible, and a deeper love for Christ.

May his memory remain as a choice possession for his congregation at Broadway Baptist Church and for a multitude of friends here in Knoxville who know and love him.

An editorial in *The Knoxville Journal* praised Dr. Pollard's "brilliant and effective ministry" which began there in 1939. *The Journal* went on to say, "There will be wide spread regret in the community by reason of the moving of Dr. Ramsey Pollard and his family to Memphis where he will become pastor of the Bellevue Baptist Church."

Dr. Pollard preached his first sermon at Bellevue on Easter Sunday, April 17, 1960. *The Bellevue Messenger* states:

Arrangements have been made to accommodate an overflow crowd. Several hundred additional seats have been provided in the Sanctuary. Latecomers will be ushered to the Lee Auditorium, where a battery of large screen television sets have been installed. All who attend will be able to participate in the Easter service as the Resurrection of our Lord is commemorated. Every Bellevue member is being called upon to be present Sunday, both morning and evening, to worship and to welcome our pastor and his lovely wife. Come to Sunday School and Training Union. Be a four-star member!!!

On Sunday night, April 24, 1960, the Bellevue congregation will have the opportunity to meet and greet the new pastor and his wife, Dr. and Mrs. Ramsey Pollard, in the friendly and relaxed atmosphere of a church reception. The lower sanctuary will be the setting for the event, and it will immediately follow the evening service.

Mr. and Mrs. Charles L. Goodall will serve as General Chairmen for the affair. They have appointed the following members to serve with them: Mrs. W. Arch Gaylor, Mrs. Carol White and Mrs. H. C. Wiseman, Mrs. William T. Howard, Mrs. Charles Householder and Dr. and Mrs. J. Cash King and Hugh Dyer.

In his column of the April 22, 1960 *Bellevue Messenger*, Dr. Pollard wrote:

Dearly Beloved, the past few days have been busy ones for us. It is quite a task to move in spite of the very wonderful service rendered by the moving firm. Thank you for your many acts of kindness. You have been most gracious in everything. We appreciate the fact that so many of you have dropped by to see us. The refreshments you brought were most helpful.

Mr. Elmer F. Bailey and Miss Velma Rhea Torbett will come to us June 1. They have been my valued associates for years, and I can assure you that Bellevue is most fortunate to secure their services. Mr. Bailey will direct all of the educational program of the church. Miss Torbett will serve as his assistant and give special attention to the Training Union work. Mrs. Bailey is a very excellent worker in Sunday School, Training Union, and WMU activities. Both Mrs. Bailey and Miss Torbett are superb singers. The Baileys have three fine boys who are looking forward to coming to Bellevue.

It will take us a while to get used to the overwhelming size of Bellevue Baptist Church, the worship center, and the marvelous Sanctuary Choir directed by Mr. Lane.

TOMMY LANE - A FRIEND AND MUSICAL MASTER

Tommy Lane and I first met at Bellevue at a children's choir festival. Choirs from all over the state were at Bellevue and the first choir to take the stage was the Bellevue Children's Choir. There were forty or more in the choir, who were beautifully robed and singing in four-part harmony. My choir from Broadway Baptist Church in Knoxville was up next with only eight children dressed in homemade robes and singing in unison. We did our best, but I felt we didn't compare to the Bellevue choir.

After the festival Mr. Lane introduced himself to me, and as he placed his arm around my shoulders, he said, "Elmer, your choir sang the most beautiful unison I have ever heard from a children's choir. I know you are proud of them." It felt wonderful to know that this great man thought we had done well. Neither of us ever dreamed of working together in years to come.

What a joy it was for me to work with him. He always encouraged me and offered to help me if I had need. We became fast friends. I have missed him over the years since he went on to Glory in 1999. Tommy had a heart for people. He visited the hospitals before other ministers could get there. He always knew when someone was in need and passed the word along to the rest of us. He gave thirty-eight years of his life to Bellevue Baptist Church as minister of music. Tommy Lane was greatly loved and he remains a sweet memory in many lives today.

BELLEVUE GOES TO THE CONVENTION

The following is an excerpt from *The Bellevue Messenger* dated May 13, 1960:

Bellevue Baptist Church holds the distinction for many "firsts" throughout her history, and is continuing making "firsts." For what other church can lay claim to the following: Having in her membership a former president of the Southern Baptist Convention, namely Dr. Robert G. Lee and Dr. Ramsey Pollard, present president, both of whom will preach for the convention in Miami: the Ladies' Quartet, composed of Mrs. Ruth Parchman, Ruth Calvert, Mrs. Frances Marks, and Frances Calvert; and the Bellevue Choir will sing for the first session of the convention. Rev. Elmer Bailey will be in charge of all music for the convention, and Bellevue Minister of Music Thomas P. Lane will assist with the singing. Now we ask you, "Can you top these firsts?"

Following a message by Billy Graham the Ladies Quartet from Bellevue will sing. Members of the choir and others will travel to the convention in Bellevue's two air-conditioned buses. We are grateful for Bellevue's contribution to the Southern Baptist Convention.

Dr. Pollard was elected by the 1960 Convention to a second term as President of the convention. The convention next year will be meeting in St. Louis, Missouri.

The Bellevue Ladies Quartet sang several times during the week. There is no doubt but that all who traveled to St. Louis for this meeting enjoyed themselves. It was a spiritual experience they will never forget.

ANOTHER RECEPTION IS ANNOUNCED

A couple of weeks later, our reception to Bellevue was announced in *The Bellevue Messenger* dated May 27, 1960:

On Sunday night, June 5, the Bellevue congregation will have an opportunity to meet the newest members of the church staff at a reception that is being planned. It will immediately follow the evening worship service.

Rev. and Mrs. Elmer Bailey and their three sons, Jimmy, Roger and Ramsey, will be here. They will be arriving in Memphis about June 1. Also, Miss Velma Rhea Torbett will arrive about the same time. Miss Torbett will be an assistant to Mr. Bailey in giving special attention to the Training Union. In charge of the reception as Co-Chairmen are Mr. and Mrs. Al Childress, and Mr. and Mrs. William B. Duncan.

It was my privilege in *The Bellevue Messenger* of June 10, 1960, to make this statement on the front page:

We have been overwhelmed with the gracious welcome Bellevue Baptists have extended to us. Dr. and Mrs. Pollard have been telling us how wonderful you are and how quickly and completely you have taken them into your fellowship with love and affection. From the moment we entered the lovely home, which you provided for us at 1160 N. Parkway Boulevard, we could feel your heart-warming hospitality. The house had been redecorated since we had last seen it with several changes and additions to add to our comfort and convenience.

Just as soon as we can get unpacked, settled and "down to earth" from the experience of moving, we wish to have open house so that we can get better acquainted with all of you. Through God's leadership and direction, you have called us and by His Spirit leading we have accepted your call. As we work together in the years to come we want to seek divine guidance and power. If we honestly and sincerely with humility of heart and singleness of purpose seek to know God's will and to do it – then we cannot help but have success in our ministry together. "If God be for us who can be against us?"

Generally speaking, my work at Bellevue Baptist Church will be to assist you and work with you in doing that which you have already been doing so successfully through the years. First of all, to reach more and more of the multitudes for Christ, winning them to a saving knowledge of Him and into fellowship with His church.

Second, our purpose shall be to teach the entire constituency of our church and all of its organizations the Word of God and to see our teaching becoming more and more efficient and effective from week to week and year to year.

Thirdly, we shall resolve to lead the membership of our great church into an intensive program of training – training in church membership through Training Union – training in specific areas of church life through the newly developed "Church Study Course for Teaching and Training" – and training through "in service" methods in all of the church organizations. Fourth, it shall be our goal to enlist a higher percentage of the membership of Bellevue into the total program of the church.

IMPLEMENTATION OF NEW SUNDAY SCHOOL PROGRAMS

At Bellevue we were less interested in methods and the strict type of organization than we had at Broadway in Knoxville. For instance, at Broadway we insisted that our teachers and officers of Sunday School participate in the Wednesday night workers meeting. At Bellevue we didn't have such a meeting of organizational workers, so we met about once a quarter for training and instructions.

During our years at Bellevue we introduced a few new strategies and organizations in Sunday School work. My wife Virginia and Mrs. Pollard were both active in providing programs for single and young married adults. Mrs. Pollard was the director of the college and career department, which effectively reached out to college students from various colleges around Memphis, and also career young adults. (Mrs. Pollard served as a conference leader at Ridgecrest and Glorieta to discuss the ministry to young adults.) My wife Virginia was director of the department for young married people. Just as the college and career departments made a big impact, the young married department had the same effect. Virginia had worked with young married people at Broadway Baptist, so she was in a unique position to give leadership to this age group at Bellevue.

The biggest change we made in Bellevue's Sunday School work was to completely reorganize the departments for preschool through sixth grade. I found this to be the most needy addition to Bellevue's Sunday School program. Our change was to eliminate small classes and provide many more departments, but to keep each department to a manageable size. This provided an opportunity for us to teach our children in a much more suitable environment and to teach them more effectively.

With all these changes, it became necessary to remodel our education building. Our children's director, Mrs. Thurman Prewett, helped lead the way as we planned for this change in our Sunday School strategy. Mrs. Tom Hight helped us redesign and redevelop the preschool area. To this day I am happy to say that our strategies are still being used in preschool and children's work.

DR. POLLARD RETIRES

Just as Lee led Bellevue through the hard times of the Great Depression, Pollard led Bellevue through the turbulent sixties. A world-shattering storm of social activism and impassioned philosophies forever altered the quality and style of American life. Many of the great institutions of the world seemed turned upside down, and many mainline protestant denominations struggled with the social gospel. Since each Baptist congregation is self-governing, it was more difficult for the social gospel to make its way into the church. At Bellevue, Pollard was a man of great courage and unimpeachable integrity, and he knew the power in preaching the inerrant Word of God.

By 1972, the sky was blue again, as it always is after a violent storm, and the "Great Constant of Bellevue" never shined brighter. One day, Dr. Pollard requested a meeting of the Committee on Committees. The committee had rarely met, and the chairman, Frank Brigance, had no idea why the pastor was calling the meeting. However, the twelve members were dutifully waiting in the parlor when Dr. Pollard arrived.

Without a lot of pomp and circumstance, Dr. Pollard announced he was retiring, and he wanted the committee to choose a Pulpit Committee to search for a pastor. He made it clear that he would not in any way interfere with the committee, and he wasn't going to make any recommendations. If the committee specifically had a person in mind and wanted his opinion, he would give it if asked. You may ask why he said this. He simply didn't want to be influential in any way in picking a new pastor of Bellevue. With that said, Pollard left the room.

The committee sat stunned. In this attractively decorated room was a magnificent portrait of Ramsey and Della Pollard, and in the equanimity of their smiles the "Great Constant of Bellevue" stirred.

I think you would be interested in reading Dr. Pollard's letter of retirement. It contains many insights into his spirit and the spirit of Bellevue when he left:

My Beloved Bellevue Congregation:

This morning (April 16, 1972) I formally announce my retirement from a pastoral ministry of 47 years. Surely you are aware that no church could lure me from this majestic pulpit and one of the greatest congregations in all the world. This message is also addressed to the multiplied thousands of television and radio friends who worship with us every week. My retirement date is June 1, 1972.

During these twelve years you have faithfully stood by me as I have sought to magnify Jesus and His Church.

The spirit of Bellevue is glorious. There is no division among our ranks. Our fellowship is unmarred by littleness, jealousy or strife. We sing "Blest Be The Tie That Binds" and we mean it. And the binding tie is our common love for our Lord and Savior, Jesus Christ.

My mistakes have been of my own making. I confess that they have been quite numerous and I thank you for your Christian charity. Whatever success has crowned our mutual ministry has largely been due to your wonderful cooperation and spirit of conquest.

My fellow Baptists have honored me with many places of great responsibility during these past thirty years. These high honors came because of my uncompromising stand for the authenticity of God's Word and the absolute necessity for an intelligent, Christ-honoring, church-centered evangelism. My fellow preachers of the Gospel are "my glory and joy."

However, the greatest honor Mrs. Pollard and I have shared is that of serving Bellevue Baptist Church during the last 9 years of our pastoral ministry. Then we would pay tribute to the Broadway Baptist Church, Knoxville, Tennessee, where we spent nearly 12 years prior to our coming to Bellevue.

It is my earnest hope that you will soon be directed to the man God has ready to succeed me. I do not know who that man is. I do know that the Holy Spirit will direct if we are submissive to His leadership. We must have God's man for the tremendous and challenging years of the future.

The incoming pastor will have my undivided support and love. If you have any criticism to offer concerning him, you will not find my heart and ears to be responsive.

The Standing Committee on Committees will nominate the proper committees to function at this critical time in the life of our beloved church.

I will spend the remaining part of my life in conducting revival meetings and related Christian activities. … Della and I thank you for your love, cooperation, and personal affection. This isn't an easy decision, but comes from an inner conviction.

God bless you now and always.
Ramsey Pollard

A few days later, the committee had solicited a few godly men and women to serve on the historic search committee – indeed they were the very embodiment of the Bellevue spirit. Albert Childress was chosen as the chairman. Others on the Pulpit Committee were Marie Armstrong, Frank Brigance, John Cameron, Bill Cochran, Mary Crawford, John Crockett, Dr. David Dunavant,

Gene Howard, Harry Johnston, Orelle Ledbetter, Roland Maddox, Morris Mills, Dr. Van Snider, Gayle Toland, and Lonnie Waters.

Soon the committee received a recommendation letter from Dr. Homer Lindsay and thus, the Bible-believing, trustworthy committee read and heard the name Adrian Rogers for the very first time.

THE CALL OF ADRIAN ROGERS

As soon as the committee began talking with Adrian Rogers, excitement started growing throughout the Bellevue family. Everyone eagerly listened to the committee's report and I distinctly remember their descriptive phrases describing Adrian Rogers. As I look back, they were clearly true, for Rogers is gifted with a presence commanding respect, just like Dr. Lee and Dr. Pollard.

Rogers' name kept popping up before the committee in unusual ways. Roland Maddox received a Sunday church program of the First Baptist Church in Merritt Island, Florida (where Rogers was pastor), from his father-in-law, Dr. O. T. Odle, who was with the Mississippi Baptists. A friend who lived in Houston, Mississippi, passed the program on to Dr. Odle because he had heard of Adrian Rogers. Chairman Al Childress' survey of growing Southeastern churches revealed that Rogers' church led in baptisms.

When the 16-member committee began scheduling visits to Merritt Island, guess who just happened to be speaking at the Baptist Pastors' Conference? Adrian Rogers! Things fell so perfectly into place, that Childress asked the committee to back off and look elsewhere. In spite of this, the members couldn't hide their enthusiasm for Rogers; they were convinced that Rogers was indeed God's man to lead Bellevue.

On August 13, 1972, Rogers preached his first sermon in the Bellevue sanctuary. There was an air of excitement throughout the service that morning. Dr. Lane then led the choir in singing "Sanctus" and the congregation joined in with the Doxology – the "Old 100th" tune from the Genevan Psalter – with words by Thomas Ken:

Praise God from Whom all blessings flow;
Praise Him, all creatures here below;
Praise Him above, ye heavenly host;
Praise Father, Son, and Holy Ghost.

At Lane's funeral twenty-seven years later, Rogers said of that day, "I'd never heard music like that before. I looked up, and the place was filled with angels. I mean God was there. God moved in on the wings of that music."

Dr. Rogers' message was straight from the Bible, and right away, the Bellevue faithful knew that he was a vigorous proponent of personal holiness and biblical inerrancy. The committee brought their report to the church and the church voted unanimously to call Dr. Adrian Rogers as pastor that very day.

Gene Howard, Chairman of the Deacons at the time, said, "Although that Sunday climaxed the search for a pastor, I believe it also marked the beginnings of greater things for Bellevue and the Lord's work in Memphis and the Mid-South. I feel our church family is ready for this tremendous challenge and the Gospel is going to be preached here as never before."

Here is what Adrian Rogers wrote in a letter to the church after his calling to Bellevue:

Dear People of Bellevue:

With deep gratitude to you for your loving confidence, with strong dependence upon the Holy Spirit, and with genuine humility I accept your invitation to be your pastor.

Your unanimous decision and overwhelming love have made indelible marks on our hearts. You are a gracious people beyond my words to express.

I am a sinner saved by grace. I marvel that God uses me, but He does. "We have this treasure in earthen vessels." Such as I am, I offer myself first to the Lord who must continually fill me with His mighty power, and then to you as your shepherd. As a good shepherd I want to spend and be spent . . . leading, feeding and protecting the flock.

Bellevue's past has been astounding. Her future can be phenomenal. I am exceedingly excited to be your pastor.

Lovingly,
Adrian Rogers

The transition between the ministry of Dr. Pollard and the ministry of Dr. Adrian Rogers was as smooth as you can imagine. Everyone agreed that they had never heard anyone articulate the truth with such conviction and zeal as Rogers. He quickly established himself as a teacher nonpareil – teaching through precisely structured messages and believing the way to grow a church is to grow a Christian. He was a sermonizer par excellence, preaching messages that disseminated the truth in ways that moved hearts and helped people.

Dr. Rogers has said many times that when he came to Bellevue, "I had a group of people who (a) loved one another, (b) believed the Bible was the Word of God, and (c) believed that the pastor is God's appointed and anointed leader. What more could a man ask?"

After Rogers became pastor, it wasn't uncommon to see Dr. Pollard pop in unexpectedly to attend a Worship Service. If Dr. Rogers was aware that Dr. Pollard was present, he usually invited him to say a word of greeting before the benediction. Dr. Pollard often had a humorous and supportive comment about what was going on at Bellevue. I remember how much he warmed our hearts with his lovable, grandfatherly manner. It was clear he was so proud of Bellevue and that he dearly loved Dr. Rogers.

As a side note, I find it interesting that Rogers preached both Lee's and Pollard's funerals. They had remained members of Bellevue Church after their retirement and had been ardent supporters and prayer warriors. There were six years when all three men – Lee, Pollard, and Rogers – were members of Bellevue Baptist Church. Pollard died in 1984 and is buried at Restland Memorial Park, Dallas, Texas.

Rogers said he spoke to Dr. Lee before his death and said, "Dr. Lee, before you go to Heaven, couldn't we take your brain and put it in my head?" Lee replied, "My boy, that would be like putting a grand piano in a closet." Although he had twinkle in his eye, Rogers wasn't sure if he was serious or not!

THE RETURN TO THE BIBLE AS
THE INFALLIBLE WORD OF GOD

Although the 1925 *Baptist Faith and Message*, declares that "the Bible has God for its author, salvation for its end, and truth without any mixture of error for its matter," by the 1960s an ecumenical drive had taken a foothold within protestant denominations. Ecumenicity was rooted in the social gospel, whereby the implementation of social legislation rather than the care of souls was the primary concern of churches.

Lee described it this way, "The ecumenical movement is horizontal and finds its authority in man – and its outreach is mostly social reform. The ministry of the true church is perpendicular, and its authority is in heaven – and its mission is to get the people ready to meet God." Nevertheless, this Protestant social gospel attitude found its way into so many Baptist churches and moderate leadership began to take over in the Southern Baptist Convention.

It wasn't long before Dr. Rogers became the leading voice for a return to the Bible as the inspired, infallible Word of God and to unashamedly proclaim that Jesus Christ is Lord, and that He alone is the answer to the longings of the human heart. The doctrine of inerrancy means that every word in the Bible is God-inspired, so that originally written, the books are error-free in every detail. Many say that Dr. Rogers is the Founding Father of the movement in the SBC to return to the infallible authority of the Word of God.

A reporter asked Rogers upon his election as president of the Southern Baptist Convention in 1979 if he believed every word in the Bible. After a pause, Rogers said, "Well, when the Bible says we are the salt of the earth, I don't believe we are sodium chloride."

In 1986, Rogers was elected to a second term and the following year he became the second three-term president of the Convention. Ever since then, the conservatives have dominated the Southern Baptist Convention. Thus the Convention's programs, including the seminaries, have systematically been transformed.

I have concluded that had it not been for the leadership of Adrian Rogers in the late 1970s, Southern Baptists doubtless would have followed the same path of spiritual decline and theological erosion evident in many of the mainline denominations. It simply would have been too late. What Rogers accomplished for Southern Baptists is one of the most remarkable achievements in American history. I have yet to find any other example of a large institution of any kind invaded with liberalism reverting to conservatism.

SUNDAY SCHOOL CHALLENGES AND PROGRAMS

When Dr. Rogers came to Bellevue, he made it clear that he didn't want to make any organizational changes during the early years of his administration. He told us, "You are doing well. God is blessing in a wonderful way and let's proceed with the program that we have."

Dr. Rogers liked what we were doing and he wanted us to just keep on doing as God would lead. In the beginning of his ministry, he said he would probably periodically inject a campaign or program for reaching people for Christ, winning them to a saving knowledge of Christ, and then leading them into involvement in the work of God in the church. His attitude helped us feel comfortable with his leadership, and we welcomed the suggestions that he wanted to make from time to time.

The staff met together regularly to plan our weekly program and Dr. Rogers was interested in knowing just what we were doing and how we were doing it. All of us on the staff learned a great deal from him and his teachings. He guided us to have a deeper prayer life and more sensitivity to the leadership of the Holy Spirit. I could feel myself growing spiritually as he taught from the Word. His sermons were magnificent. God gave him a power of communicating the truth of the Word like no other man. He had all of us eating out of his hand.

After only a few months. Dr. Rogers set a goal for Bellevue to have 2,000 on average in Bible Study. This was quite a goal for us for we had been running around 1,600 when he arrived. In a short time we broke that 2,000 barrier and once again he challenged us to reach the 5,000 mark. This was a big challenge and one that taxed us to find ideas.

In staff meeting he challenged us and suggested many things that we knew how to do, but we had just been coasting. We started putting into practice the philosophies of church growth that we knew. We encouraged the members of our church who were not enrolled in Sunday School to start attending. After several weeks, we enlarged our scope outside church and began taking surveys of people who lived in our area. We visited and cultivated friendships with these people, and God blessed in a wonderful way by leading many of them to join Sunday School and the church.

In the fall of 1975 we had an emphasis one Sunday morning called "Feeding of the 5000." Bellevue Boulevard, the street that ran in front of the church, was closed that morning and traffic was diverted so that we could set up chairs, choir risers, and a podium for the pastor to speak. People came from everywhere. The air was charged with excitement and expectancy as we gathered outdoors for a wonderful worship experience. It was a never-to-be-forgotten time for the more than 5,400 who attended. (At that time we were averaging just over 2,500 in Bible Study attendance.) On this special day, the music was thrilling, the sermon was challenging, and the crowd was blessed. Many who were there continue to talk about this grand day in the life of our church. Souls were reached, lives were changed, and Jesus was glorified. It gave a new spark to our Bible Study efforts.

In October 1981, Dr. Rogers suggested we have a "Body of Christ Day." An artist from our church drew an outline of the body of Christ with outstretched arms on a parking lot across from the church. On "Body of Christ" Sunday, all the departments and classes of the church filed onto the parking lot in a designated order and filled the outline. Then, a photographer took a picture of this remarkable sight from a helicopter (the picture was used many times for future campaigns). God blessed in a remarkable way that Sunday. His Spirit came down on us, and on that day we had more than 5,100 in Sunday School.

In a short time our average attendance reached nearly 4,000 and Dr. Rogers asked us to accept the next big challenge to raise that average attendance to 6,000. WOW! This was a huge commitment. But, as he said, "With God everything is possible." If He could take us from an average of 1,600 to 4,000, it would be no trouble for Him to reach 6,000.

Some time during these years, Dr. Rogers suggested we not call Sunday School by the traditional name anymore, but call it Bible Study Fellowship instead. He felt the name "Sunday School" was overworked and we needed a fresh outlook and vision. We didn't really change anything we were doing, we simply highlighted the primary need for fellowship in the Bible Study hour. All of the classes had an opportunity every Sunday for a time of fellowship followed by a lesson presented by the teacher.

At the time, I thought our pastor was surely a miracle man, but truly he was just a man of God, humbly appealing to the people to do what they should be doing in witnessing, winning souls, helping people grow in Christ, and thereby growing themselves. He constantly emphasized the need for Bible study and prayer.

So, combining the new idea of Sunday School now being Bible Study Fellowship and the glory and worship and praise that emanated from the choir and the music ministry, the attendance patterns in Bible Study Fellowship today have grown to 8,000 and sometimes reaching the 9,000 mark.

MUSIC MINISTRY GROWTH UNDER JIM WHITMIRE

Four years after Dr. Rogers arrived, Bellevue Baptist called Jim Whitmire as minister of youth music. He had served with Dr. Rogers for several years at Merritt Island Baptist Church and was their minister of music at the time of his call to Bellevue. Dr. Rogers had mentioned on several occasions Jim's wonderful music capabilities and how creative he was in planning musical productions, but he assured us the most important characteristic of Jim was his walk with the Lord. Indeed, Jim was a superb musician, a well-informed educator, and had a warm Christian personality. He was also an astute Bible scholar, particularly in what the Bible had to say about music. Jim saw the musicians in the church as the Levites of the Old Testament, the ones who were the leaders in praise and worship. When he arrived, he announced that his goal was to teach and train the choir to be ministers of music and take the part which the Levites played in the Old Testament.

Soon after Jim arrived, he organized the youth for the first Singing Christmas Tree performance. It was a miniature in comparison to the magnificent productions of today. Even without all of the sets, lights, and stage props that we have now, that small production opened the eyes of people to what could be done. From this small beginning came not only The Singing Christmas Tree, but also Celebrate America, Living Pictures, and the famed Memphis Passion Play.

As Jim Whitmire's work progressed, talent seemed to come out of the woodwork. For years instrumentalists from other churches or the Memphis Symphony helped us with the special productions, but before long Bellevue members filled every seat in the orchestra. My wife Virginia became a prime helper in the major productions by writing scripts, directing the casts, and choreographing the singers. She had little training, but a lot of natural talent.

When Tommy Lane retired as minister of music Jim Whitmire was promoted to take his place. During his years as minister of youth music, Jim hoped that one day God's plan would include him becoming Bellevue's minister of music. Under Jim's leadership a miracle of marriage took place between the music, education, ministerial, and evangelism divisions of the church. Before, it seemed these departments were in competition with one another – each trying to outdo the other in programming making it difficult for the kind of teamwork that was needed. It took a while for people to understand what Jim was trying to do, but soon they began to see the wisdom and spiritual vision of unity, which Jim wanted for all the Bellevue programs.

The basis of Jim's philosophy was stated in *The Church Musician* (July 2000), a publication of Lifeway Resources. It quoted him as saying:

Like all church programs, growth is essential to music ministries. To have a living ministry a minister of music has to plant, water, and grow musicians – the principles I use to build a music ministry to fit the needs in any size church. I think God will hold us accountable for the people we do not teach, or at least offer to teach.

As I began organizing the multitude of notes about Bellevue's music ministry random praises from Platgree's stanza to "When In Our Music God is Glorified" kept parading like brilliant banners across the platform of my mind, heralding various aspects of their ministry to help us to envision it. I flagged various divisions with praises from the majestic hymn to highlight the purpose, achievements, goals and resources that depict this great church's extraordinary music ministry.

THE BIRTH OF THE BELLEVUE PERFORMING ARTS

Jim has an unusual ability to see the hidden talents in people, and he seeks to bring these talents into perspective. Over the years, parents continue to grab at the chance to have their children trained in violin, harp, bells, and other instruments through the church's Performing Arts Center. This unique ministry offers quality music instruction with a Christian perspective. Specific lessons are offered weekly in flute, clarinet, bassoon, saxophone, trumpet, French horn, trombone, baritone, piano, organ, and voice.

In 1983, Carter Threlkeld, was called as Bellevue's minister of instrumental music. He conducts the orchestra and leads the band and Performing Arts Center programs. Carter Threlkeld's dream has always been to make "music with a mission" – going to the streets and wherever else the Lord leads to bring others to a saving knowledge of the Lord Jesus Christ. His three-fold goal is to teach people to worship, to live a witness, and to lead in worship.

The Beginning Band is a learning center to grow musicians for bands that follow. Beginning Band is for any student in the fifth grade and up who has never had lessons or band experience. Victory Marching Band is comprised of the Intermediate Blue (sixth graders and up), the Intermediate Red (seventh and eighth graders), and Advanced Band (ninth through twelfth graders with at least two years of band or private lessons).

All the bands are avenues in which the Gospel can be presented to people in the street. Recitals are common throughout the year and the string program has an annual graduation. There is also a solo ensemble festival for anyone involved in the Performing Arts Center or band program. In this festival students play or sing before a judge for a rating. Because of the exceptional Performing Arts Center teaching program, Bellevue has not had to hire any musicians for many years.

The most remarkable thing about this music program has been its impact on evangelism. All of the different ensemble groups witness on the streets, in senior citizens residences, hospitals, and jails. Thousands have been won to Christ through these activities.

In the four annual productions each year an invitation is given at the close of each performance. In 2001, over three thousand people made professions of faith at the conclusion of the Memphis Passion Play and over two thousand people made professions of faith after the Singing Christmas Tree performances. Over the last twenty-plus years, more than eight-seven thousand people have accepted Christ as their Savior at these and other productions.

REFLECTIONS UPON THE HISTORY OF BELLEVUE: FROM MISSION TO MAGNIFICENT

A long time ago, someone wrote, "The history of Bellevue Baptist Church could be written in four words – From Mission to Magnificent." Let me close this chapter with some historical treasures about the history of Bellevue. I'd like to thank Jim Pirtle of Bellevue who has written an extensive document on Bellevue's history. I credit him with much of the following information, and much the preceding.

Back in 1898, God placed a vision and a burden on the heart of Dr. Thomas S. Potts, pastor of the Central Baptist Church, which was located at Beale and South Second streets, to establish a mission "way out from the downtown area."

A three-member committee was appointed, and the chairman, Jesse O'Dell, rode his bicycle to look over a site on the northeast corner of Bellevue Avenue and Erskine Street that someone had suggested. At that time, Erskine was an unpaved street without any houses (later it was renamed Court Street).

Dr. Potts led the construction of a little stone church at a cost of approximately $3,500, of which $1,000 came from a gift by a widow named Mrs. Fanny Jobe. The mission was dedicated on Sunday, July 12, 1903, with Dr. H. P. Hurt installed as the first pastor. By August 9, Dr. Hurt had secured 32 charter members and the church was constituted as Bellevue Avenue Baptist Church. Shortly thereafter, "Avenue" was dropped and from then on, the little stone church was known as Bellevue Baptist Church.

At the time, most of Bellevue's members lived within walking distance. Those who lived farther away rode streetcars, which conveniently stopped nearby. Parking didn't become a matter of concern until the 1940s.

In 1914, Hurt resigned and Dr. R. M. Inlow became the pastor for the next seven years. Soon after the arrival of the third pastor, Dr. H. W. Bostick in 1921, the congregation outgrew the little stone church. The impressive new structure that was dedicated in 1924 later became known as Lee Auditorium.

In the 1950s, Bellevue became the largest Southern Baptist church east of the Mississippi River with more than 9,000 members. In 1952, Bellevue completed their magnificent sanctuary in the midtown location, which seated nearly 3,000 persons. One of the very first air-conditioned churches in Memphis, the majestic building was an architectural masterpiece inspiring in its beauty, and a powerful magnet for attracting people to Jesus. A beautiful chandelier hung gracefully from the ceiling of the sanctuary, and on the podium was a new custom-made, finely crafted pulpit.

Beginning on January 5, 1958, Bellevue became the first church in the United States to telecast with its own equipment on WHBQ-TV. For the next two decades, hundreds and thousands watched Lee and Pollard on the television.

Bellevue's membership, however, remained fixed. Sunday School attendance declined noticeably because of the suburban flight of young families into outlying subdivisions. Many had hoped to continue attending Bellevue worship services, but in the end, the long drive was too demanding. You may wonder why a drive from suburbia to midtown was so much, but let me remind you that during the 1950s, most cars didn't have air conditioning and expressways hadn't been built yet.

Even though Bellevue's Sunday School attendance dropped, Bellevue's steadfast spirit had not weakened in any way. In looking back, I can see that God used these years to temper Bellevue in much the same way as metal is tempered to make a fine sword.

By the end of the 1970s, the expressway system was complete, which made it possible for people in the Greater Memphis area to have easy access to the church. Many members, including some who had left under traumatic circumstance, began to visit, and one by one they rejoined the Bellevue fellowship.

During these years, Bellevue's midtown location aided its ministry tremendously. Three major funeral homes and the Memphis Medical Center were just blocks away. My wife, Virginia was director of hostesses at Baptist Memorial Hospital for 30 years, and she kept Bellevue's staff so well posted that one time before an expectant father had arrived, he was astonished to learn that the pastor had already been there.

In 1977, Bellevue began having two worship services. Within a few more years, a third service was required. Bellevue was quickly outgrowing its facilities in midtown Memphis. In 1983, the church voted to purchase more than 370 acres at Appling Road and Interstate 40 for a new campus. Pastor Rogers dubbed it Canaan, and in July, 1987, a groundbreaking ceremony took place unlike any I had ever seen. When a gigantic earthmoving machine popped up out of nowhere, I jumped to my feet.

On New Year's Eve 2000, the landmark 150-foot monument featuring three crosses in gleaming white steel were dedicated at the expressway intersection. The Fellowship Building was dedicated January 14, 2001 as the final major component of the Master Plan.

Bellevue's impressive campus in Cordova has facilities built to last a hundred years. To accommodate the needs of its membership, Bellevue has almost a half million square feet of building space. But, while these breathtaking buildings reflect the highest aspirations of the Bellevue dream, they are for the glory of God and the winning of souls. Indeed, Bellevue is a place of worship for the 21st century. Churches are no longer places where people merely go to worship on Sunday. They are now centers where spiritual, social, physical, and emotional needs can be met through seminars, family activities, classes and support groups.

Today, Bellevue's membership is approximately 28,000 under Rogers, who is the most renowned expositor of God's Word in Christendom today. In addition, he is the model preacher for world evangelism. Through Love Worth Finding Ministries, which began in 1987, Dr. Rogers' messages are broadcast on more than 1,100 radio and 14,000 television outlets in four languages in more than 150 countries.

WHY BELLEVUE IS SUCH A GREAT CHURCH

People are always asking, "Why is Bellevue such a great church?" I can say without any equivocation whatsoever that Bellevue is a great church because of the three wonderful pastors over the last seventy-four years – Dr. Robert G. Lee, Dr. Ramsey Pollard, and Dr. Adrian Rogers.

R. G. Lee pastored Bellevue from 1927 to 1960, then Ramsey Pollard pastored the church throughout the 1960s and he laid the foundation in 1972 for Adrian Rogers. (Bellevue is the only church to have had three consecutive pastors selected to head the Southern Baptist Convention.) These Christ-honoring men believed fervently in the inerrancy of the Scriptures – preaching that the Bible provides the only basis for living the Christian life. While Lee had revolutionized preaching with his pictorial style of delivering sermons filled with life and color; Pollard held fast to his topical sermons properly called for during the sixties. I think of Pollard as a veteran captain who used the Bible as his guide and piloted the ship Bellevue through a very bad storm into the safety of a snug harbor.

As for Dr. Rogers, he has his own style of faithfully and lovingly teaching a profound knowledge of Jesus Christ and understanding of God's Word. I believe out of Dr. Rogers' many outstanding messages from God's Word, none is more splendid than his sermon "The Blood Covenant," which he delivered with such extraordinary grace that it touched the core of one's being when I first heard it. Based on 2 Samuel 9, the sermon is an applicable portrayal of the lovingkindness of God to His people from the story of King David and Mephiboseth.

Still another reason Bellevue is such a great church is its large extended family that includes great pastors such as Dr. Lindsay who wrote the letter recommending Dr. Rogers and Dr. W.A. Criswell of the First Baptist Church of Dallas, Texas, and legions of lay people at Memphis and around the world.

Through the years, Bellevue has been blessed by scores of dedicated deacons and workers. I am happy to point out that several deacons from years gone by are still active, and I will always regard Morris Mills as Bellevue's chairman of the board emeritus. Emily Wilson has taught a Sunday School class for more than sixty years. Steadfastness is a mark of many Bellevue members. Often, when members move away and return for a visit, they feel as if they have never been gone.

Final Thoughts At The Time Of This Writing

Several descendants of the Founding Fathers of Bellevue are members today, including Mrs. Grace Turner, a great-granddaughter of Dr. Potts, and Gordon Hollingsworth, a grandson of Willis Henry Hollingsworth. Mr. Hollingsworth served on Bellevue's site-finding committee and he was a charter member.

Bellevue is contemplating its centennial celebration, and there is excitement in the air. Longtime members look forward to many more golden years. Under the helm of the youthful 70-year old Rogers, the Bellevue ship of state sails into its second century extraordinarily prepared to spread the Christian Gospel throughout the Western Hemisphere and to the ends of the Earth.

The founder and longtime teacher of the Pioneer Bible Class, Dr. David Dunavant, always summed his lesson up in one sentence, so I cannot think of one sentence more apropos than this to end this chapter: "Bellevue is a testimony to the Bible."

CHAPTER ELEVEN

THE PASSING OF MY PRECIOUS JEWEL

In 1986 Virginia was diagnosed with bone marrow cancer and underwent chemotherapy treatments for the next year. Thankfully, the chemotherapy treatment was not difficult for Virginia. She didn't have much sickness or nausea from it and came through it very well. In fact, she worked every day during that year to develop and write a program for volunteers at Baptist Hospital. She visited many hospitals with good volunteer programs to determine the best way to set up such a program at Baptist.

Before Virginia's volunteer program, Baptist Memorial Hospital didn't have any volunteers. Instead, they had paid hostesses who were recent graduates of Baptist universities. They provided excellent care of the non-medical needs of the patients, but it was a very costly service. After Dr. Frank Groner retired (he was not only president of the hospital, but he also founded the hostess program), the program was discontinued. Virginia's volunteer program was implemented that year she was taking chemotherapy.

How thrilled we were when at the end of that period, the doctor informed us that the cancer had gone into remission. There were no cancer cells in her body! Sadly, our good news was short-lived. After just a short remission, the cancer came back with a vengeance. She was put on radiation treatments and almost immediately she began to feel the treatments were not right for her.

One night, she came home after taking part in her last Singing Christmas Tree at Bellevue, and told me she had a terrible pain in her sternum. She thought the cancer had returned and went to see Dr. Kirby Smith the next day. The test results were positive. The cancer had come back. The radiation treatments tackled the spot on her sternum, but the cancer immediately went to one of her shoulders. Treatments were then done on her shoulder, then it moved somewhere else. This was the pattern for several months.

The doctors were doing the best they knew to do, yet I could see my precious Virginia was going downhill with each treatment. She began to have hallucinations because of pain medication, which kept her out of pain most of the time. The radiation treatments continued, but she grew weaker and weaker. Before she got sick, she enjoyed walking the halls of the hospital and talking to people. After the treatments, she used a walker and would walk as far as she could. Soon she could not get out of bed and had trouble communicating with us, but she did talk to God. She was constantly praying that God would take her home. I remember hearing her pray, "Oh, Lord, take me home. I can't live with this."

I stayed by her side at night and early in the morning I would help feed her and get her freshened up for the day. I would then go to the office and work until about 4 in the afternoon, go home for supper, and back to the hospital to spend the night. Virginia had lots of company during the day. Some of her friends and girls who worked for her would often relieve me in the early morning so I could go home to shower and shave. The staff of the church, including Dr. Rogers, were all gracious to help us, as well. Julia and Betty, our daughter-in-laws, were very helpful as much as their work would permit.

Weeks later Virginia seemed to be more alert than usual. She was trying so hard to be brave. Julia, my daughter-in-law, was visiting Virginia, and they insisted that I go out and get a good meal. They twisted my arm, and I kissed Virginia, gave her a good hug, and told her I loved her. While I was gone, Virginia died. Julia and Jody said she didn't struggle at the last but gave a sigh and smiled a sweet smile. When I got to the room, I noticed the smile was still there. When she died, she must have seen something wonderful. I wonder if she had a glimpse of glory and saw Jesus face-to-face. Probably He was saying to her, "Well done, my dear child. Enter into this place I have prepared for you." I then prayed, "Oh, God, my Father, I thank You that You have answered Virginia's prayers. No more suffering, no more pain, no more cancer. All is well. Praise God."

Oh, what sweet memories I have of our life together. What would I have done without her, the precious pearl God gave to me. If you're looking from heaven, thanks Virginia for all the wonderful opportunities we had for service to God through our forty-nine and a half years together. God is great!

Just as Jesus grieved at the death of Lazarus, I grieved for the loss of my Virginia. God soothed my heart and mind and gave me a peace that passed all understanding. Death for one who was suffering like Virginia was a release and our prayers were answered. Psalm 116:15 says, "Precious in the sight of the LORD, is the death of His saints." To God be the glory!

RETIREMENT YEARS IN CHURCH CONSULTING

In the Spring of 1981, I was critically ill in the hospital with a bacterial infection for some time. As I was recuperating, God's Spirit started moving in my heart. I felt Him calling me to a retirement ministry as a church growth consultant. This was a very exciting time for me. For the next ten years I was invited to conduct church growth conferences in 292 churches. Some were one-day conferences, others lasted two to three days. Sometimes I spent a longer time consulting with churches, and these appeared to be the most profitable. I was graciously received by churches all over the country.

For instance, for six years I helped Germantown Baptist Church develop a multi-level staff of church administrators. Dr. Ken Storey was the pastor during these years. When he first went there, the membership and facilities were small. He and the secretary were the only church staff. During the eighties Germantown experienced a rapid growth of baby boomer singles and marrieds. Year by year Germantown Baptist grew right along with the community and added staff and enlarged classes.

What a challenge this was to me – an opportunity to help a pastor who was conscious of the fact that he needed help. I felt from the very beginning that this was going to be a very interesting and profitable experience. And it truly was.

My first few weeks at Germantown Baptist were spent studying the church membership and attendance records, the Sunday School program, and the staff of the church. The staff didn't have job descriptions. Everyone was doing what they thought was the right thing, but they needed a direction that was common to all. Also, the church didn't have a mission statement or anyone supervising this large staff. The pastor had fallen into the trap of doing everything, rather than designating the work to the various staff members. This wasn't from a selfish standpoint, but from a standpoint of rapid growth. My work was cut out for me, and I felt that God would give me the wisdom to help them get on track. After many sessions with Brother Storey, I turned my attention to the leadership of the church, including the staff and laity.

Brother Storey gave instructions to the staff members concerning my place as a consultant. He urged them to listen carefully to me and to take notes on what I had to say, as well as to follow the suggestions which I would make. Some of the staff resisted some of the things I said because they didn't understand, but as we worked and prayed together, they came to be a very cooperative group.

I asked each staff member to give me a list of all the things that they did in the priority of importance. I then asked them to list some things that they didn't like to do and felt should not be in their job description. We set a deadline for when these lists would be completed and turned in to me. These lists would help me draw up job descriptions and organize the staff.

I was amazed at what an excellent job the staff did of relating the things they did. After I analyzed all of this information, I developed an organization plan, plus suggestions for job descriptions. I made it clear that I was only suggesting these job descriptions, which they would discuss with the pastor.

Throughout the process, I worked closely with Brother Storey and I think he began to clearly see the directions he needed to take in order to serve as the pastor of a multi-staff church.

I conducted a meeting with the staff in which I reminded them of the situation their church was facing. I listed some things that they should consider if they wanted to continue growing at the rate which they were growing. The first item had to do with lay leadership. Their Sunday School and Church Training needed training for new workers. A program of training was planned and put into effect. The second item was a need for more space. I didn't need to tell them that they needed space, but I emphasized that they couldn't start new units of Sunday School, Church Training, and more without space. They were effectively using every bit of space they had, so they found off-campus space to rent or use without charge.

After I thought I had completed my work at Germantown, Brother Storey asked me to stay as staff coordinator until they could find a permanent person. I was with them several years, and it was a wonderful experience for me. They took my recommendations and went forward with them and began to grow like kudzu.

Another long-term consultation was with First Baptist Church, West Memphis, Arkansas. When I joined them, they were in a building program to provide more space for education. They asked me to advise them during the planning stages of this project. I believe I helped them to avoid some serious mistakes during those two years. When I left, they had a beautiful facility to take care of their projected growth.

A third long-term consultation was with First Baptist Church, Pensacola, Florida. They were without a pastor or educational director, and they asked me to help them keep their program going. This was another blessing that God gave me to work with such fine people. God blessed the time I spent with them by helping us turn their Sunday School around from a static condition to a growing situation.

I think that probably the most exciting church growth consultation I had was with the Audubon Park Baptist Church in Memphis at a time when they were contemplating merging with Park Avenue Baptist Church. I had never gone through the experience of helping two churches merge, but I sought wisdom from Dr. Pollard and Dr. Howard Kolb, who was the pastor of Audubon Park Baptist Church.

My personal goal in that consultation was to make sure that there were not vestiges of power structures from the two churches that would cause division down the line. This wasn't an easy problem to solve, for both churches had ideas that would lead to problems in the future unless we effectively worked them out in the beginning. I advised them to have complete separation from the organization of their churches and merge into one.

Both groups wanted to maintain their separate deacon membership and Sunday School classes. This would have been disastrous. To resolve the Sunday School problem, I suggested they completely reorganize the combined Sunday School program. Neither church had a semblance of grading in the adults, so I suggested that they study the ages of everyone in the classes, then project a plan for grading people from both Audubon Park Church and Park Avenue Church. They did a fairly good job, but it wasn't perfect. I didn't expect that it would be, but the result of the merger was very successful.

The most unusual consultation I had was with Mt. Pisgah Baptist Church in Spartanburg, South Carolina. When I arrived at the church I was amazed.

The church building was a little country church building that was located in the front of a huge cemetery. The church didn't own the cemetery, they just owned their church building.

They were locked in for parking; the only parking was in the driveways of the cemetery. They had an arrangement with the cemetery that there would be no burials on Sundays. This allowed plenty of space for parking, but much of it was far from the little church building. The first Sunday I was there, they had about 400 in the congregation and the little church was packed. Rev. Fred Lowrey was anxious for his church to grow, but I knew that was impossible where it was located.

My first recommendation to them was to move their church away from the cemetery, but stay in North Spartanburg. I also recommended that they change the name of the church from Mt. Pisgah to North Spartanburg Baptist Church. Finally, I suggested ideas for a building and what they would need to do in programming to grow their church.

Fred Lowrey tried twice to encourage the church to change its name and move to another area, but the congregation turned him down both times. Fred eventually felt his work at that church was complete, and he accepted a call with the First Baptist Church of Bossier City, Louisiana (it is a fine, fast-growing church).

A new pastor came on the scene at Mt. Pisgah and eventually led the people to accept my recommendations. They began to grow, and they are now a much larger church, having thousands in attendance. God really blessed me in that I didn't know what to do when I arrived at that church, but He led me every step of the way and all the glory and credit goes to Him. I was just a happy participant.

My years in church growth consulting work were happy and busy years. There was a lot of travel, study, and prayer that went with it. It wasn't easy, but it was very productive, and I am grateful for those years. I learned a great deal as I visited these different churches. I saw things they were doing that were new to me and I added some of these features to my program. I found that I didn't have a corner on church growth. I knew a little bit about it and had great deal of experience in it, but I found there were a lot of things being done out there that were different from the way I worked.

Now, I decided it was time to truly retire. My retirement wasn't from the ministry, but rather from Church Growth Basics, my company. What have I done to take up my time during these post-retirement years? Well, first of all Ramsey Pollard Jr. asked me to help him with his talk show on tourism entitled "Ramblin' with Ramsey," where he broadcasts from some exotic place every week. He asked me to be a host to the broadcast.

I would intercept his guests as they arrived since he was confined to a microphone and broadcasting equipment. I would receive them, seat them, get their names and place their card with information about them on Ramsey's desk so he would know who was there. These would not only include people to watch a broadcast, but also invited guests who would be interviewed on the air by Ramsey. Mostly, they were executives of hotels, motels, and tourism sites. I traveled with him about three times a month. Sometimes not as often, but it gave me something to do and opportunities to be in places I never would have been able to see all over this country. I enjoyed my time as a volunteer and Ramsey took care of my meals and lodging wherever we went. It was lots of fun, and I still go with him now and then.

OPPORTUNITIES TO SERVE IN THE
CHOIR AND SUNDAY SCHOOL

Probably the most enjoyable experience of these post-retirement years has been the opportunity I have had to serve as a volunteer in my own church, Bellevue Baptist Church. I taught a men's Sunday School class for several years, and now I am still a member and direct the music at the beginning of the class each Sunday. I also have the privilege of participating in the music program as a member of the Sanctuary Choir and I must say that choir rehearsals are far more than rehearsals. They are sweet times of meditation and prayer, as well. I often come away from choir rehearsal with rejoicing in my heart and a renewal in my soul.

It has also been my privilege over the years to participate in the Passion Play in the role of the rabbi who marries the couple just before Jesus turns the water into wine. I have also sung in the Singing Christmas Tree and served as a host for the event, playing the part of master of ceremonies.

One of my biggest thrills has been to take part in a children's musical, Noah and the Ark. I played the part of Noah and Tommy Lane played the part of Noah's conscience. It was a lot of fun and a good production.

Even before my taking part in these productions, my wife Virginia and I always enjoyed music. Right after we were married we started singing duets for church, Sunday School classes, banquets, and parties. We had lots of fun with it and received sweet blessings.

In the realm of fun music, Virginia suggested that we do segments from "Fiddler On the Roof." She sang the song which Goldie, the wife of Reb Tevye sang and I sang the songs of Reb Tevye. We started doing this while we were at Broadway Baptist and when we came to Bellevue we carried on the tradition. I don't know how many times we sang "A Night With the Fiddler." We were a very popular duo.

Virginia also played a role in the early years of The Singing Tree; in fact, she played the role of a grandmother in a good many of the programs until 1989. After she died I decided to carry on "The Fiddler On the Roof" program, by singing solos from the musical. I can't count the number of times I have sung this, and I still do it every once in awhile.

I thank God every day for all of the wonderful opportunities He gave me through the years in education and music, and for the chance to work with other churches in my consulting days. I also praise God for the blessings He gave me to work with Ramsey Pollard, Jr., and participate in the ministry of the great Bellevue Baptist Church where I served as education director for 21 years.

God has truly been good to Elmer Bailey.

BENEDICTION

I pray that you have. . . .

Joy - unspeakable and full of glory.

Peace - that surpasses understanding.

Success - in each facet of your life.

Friends - sent from God.

Love - everlasting.

Knowledge - that ye may not perish.

Special memories - of all that the Lord has done.

A rejoiceful day - that the Lord has made.

A path - that leads to the blessings of God.

Dreams - that become realities.

Appreciation - for all that God has made you.

Author unknown